ENDORSEMENTS

'This book is a winner, full of tremendous wisdom which will surely help many, many people on their spiritual path.'

Eileen Caddy
Author of *Opening Doors Within*,
co-founder of the Findhorn Community

'David's clear and lucid guidance shows us how to link to the Angelic realms for ourselves. He is the perfect guide to the company of Angels.'

Judy Hall
Author of *The Art of Psychic Protection*

'David Lawson writes like a gardening Angel, feet firmly rooted in the earth and face turned towards the heavenly sun. He addresses the Angelic in all of us.'

Kitty Campion
Author of *Holistic Woman's Herbal*

'David Lawson takes you on a healing journey that everyone can benefit from.'

Louise L. Hay
Author of *You Can Heal Your Life*

OTHER BOOKS BY DAVID LAWSON

Money and Your Life — A Prosperity Play Book (with Justin Carson). Published by Healing Workshops Press.

I See Myself in Perfect Health — A Visualisation for Health Book. Published by Healing Workshops Press.

Star Healing — Your Sun Sign, Your Health and Your Success. Published by Hodder & Stoughton (Headway).

I See Myself In Perfect Health — Your Essential Guide to Self Healing. Published by Thorsons (HarperCollins).

Principles of Self-healing. Published by Thorsons (HarperCollins).

So You Want to be a Shaman. Published by Godsfield Press in the UK and Conari Press in the US.

Principles of Your Psychic Potential. Published by Thorsons (HarperCollins).

The Eye of Horus — An Oracle of Ancient Egypt. Published by St. Martin's Press (US), Connections (UK), Simon & Schuster (Australia), Solar (France) and De Kern (The Netherlands).

AUDIO TAPES

Money and Your Life — A Prosperity Course (with Justin Carson). Published by Healing Workshops Press.

I See Myself in Perfect Health — Volume One. Published by Healing Workshops Press.

I See Myself in Perfect Health — Volume Two. Published by Healing Workshops Press.

A Company of Angels

Your Angel Transformation Guide

By David Lawson

FINDHORN
Press

First published in 1998

ISBN 1 899171 02 9

British Library Cataloguing-in-Publication Data.
A catalogue record for this book is available from the British Library.

Layout by Pam Bochel
Front cover illustration by Tilia and Peter Weevers
Author's photograph by Michael Wildsmith
Cover design by Thierry Bogliolo

Printed and bound by WSOY, Finland

Published by

Findhorn Press

The Park, Findhorn,
Forres IV36 0TZ
Scotland
Tel +44 (0)1309 690582/Fax 690036
e-mail: books@findhorn.org
http://www.findhorn.org/findhornpress/

DEDICATION

This book is dedicated to all of the Angels in my life, past and present. There have been many.

This book is also specially dedicated to the memory of my Grandpa, Ron Tyler — an Angel who had the luck of the Devil.

With love, David.

ABOUT THE AUTHOR

David Lawson is an English healer, writer and course leader. Together with partner Justin Carson he travels the world teaching self-healing techniques, hands-on healing, psychic development and spiritual growth.

His books include *Star Healing — Your Sun Sign, Your Health and Your Success* (Hodder & Stoughton), *Money and Your Life — A Prosperity Playbook* (with Justin Carson: Healing Workshops Press), *So You Want to be a Shaman* (Godsfield Press — UK, Conari — USA), *I See Myself in Perfect Health — Your Essential Guide to Self Healing*, *Principles of Self Healing* and *Principles of Your Psychic Potential* (Thorsons). He is perhaps best known for his book and divination pack based upon the gods and goddesses of the Egyptians, *The Eye of Horus — An Oracle of Ancient Egypt* (Connections — UK, St. Martin's Press — USA, Simon & Schuster — Australia).

David is an authorised worldwide facilitator of the *You Can Heal Your Life* study course programme, based upon the work of Louise L. Hay with whom he studied. David is a natural intuitive, a hands-on healer, a counsellor and an expert in divination techniques such as the Tarot, Astrology and his own *Eye of Horus* stone tablets. Over the past twelve years he has helped many people to transform their lives through his books, audio tapes, workshops and one-to-one sessions.

A regular broadcaster, David has contributed to a number of television and radio shows. He has recently appeared on GMTV, ITN News, Channel Five and Sky One in the UK and Channel Nine and Channel Ten in Australia.

'David Lawson takes you on a healing journey that everyone can benefit from.' Louise L. Hay, author of *You Can Heal Your Life*.

For details of David Lawson's courses, books and audio tapes, please write to Healing Workshops, PO Box 1678, London, NW5 4EW, UK, or e-mail at healingwps@aol.com

CONTENTS

ACKNOWLEDGEMENTS

I would like to thank the following people for their help in the writing and publication of this book:

Susan Mears, Thierry Bogliolo, Karin Bogliolo, Judy Hall, Eileen Caddy, Lynn Barton, Pam Bochel, Tilia and Peter Weevers, Lilian and Eric Lawson, Anne and Alex Carson, Stephanie Holland, David Morton, Jessica West-Ramakrishnan, Sue Bowes, Jo Neary, Dorianne Beyer, Francesca Mereu, Roberta Simoni, Caroline Scattergood, Lena Davis, Kate Levy, the delicious Kitty Campion and all of my friends, family, clients and guides.

Special thanks to Louise L. Hay for her inspiration and encouragement and also to my partner Justin Carson whose practical support, ideas, good humour and care make it possible for me to write.

David Lawson

London — 30th April 1998

Prologue
Where Angels Dwell

by Judy Hall

As a karmic astrologer and past life regression therapist, I inhabit diverse time frames and move between different levels of consciousness to facilitate personal growth. For almost twenty-five years I have guided clients into other lives and the 'between life state'. My exploration has taken me into many realms beyond the physical. The only way I have found to categorise these different realms is to say that they exist at different vibrational frequencies — the earth plane being an extremely dense level, and the more spiritual planes having a much lighter vibration. I see all of creation as existing on multitudinous levels. We are aware of much of creation in our everyday life: we interact with our fellow creatures; we gaze at the stars; we take in the warmth of the sun. But there are levels that are usually invisible to us. Until, that is, we take time to make contact.

It has become clear to me that subtle energies surround us all the time. These energies manifest, for instance, as our astrological chart, a 'cosmic imprint' of our moment of birth that maps past, present and future. It shows the credits and deficits that accrue to us across time. The subtle energies also show themselves in our aura, that invisible energy field that surrounds and protects our physical body — a field which also reflects our karmic inheritance. The subtlest levels interpenetrate not only this life as we are living it now, on the earth plane, but also many other levels of being. It is these energies that make possible our communication with the different vibrations.

For the most part, these other levels of being are unrecognised and known only to a comparative few. In regression, most people naturally gravitate to other lives (usually, but not always, experienced as 'in the past'). Some explore the between life state with its healing and wisdom dimensions. A few merge back into the wholeness of the light levels from which we all emerged and to which we will all return. An even smaller number will explore other realms entirely. In meditation, much the same thing can happen, quite spontaneously. We either go 'in' to make contact with our deeper selves or 'out' to contact the other realms. An astrological chart too can be read from many perspectives.

It is this unfolding of worlds within worlds and of the different realms of existence that makes my work so fascinating. I have regressed hundreds of people, studied at least a thousand astrological charts and explored healing in its widest context. I have prescribed subtle vibrational remedies for ills both ancient and modern, 'reframed' past traumas and connected clients to unused potential. What has linked the disparate facets of my work has been higher guidance. I have worked with the other realms for so long now that I take their presence for granted. But it is always a potent moment when a client connects with higher energies. I recognise that as a point at which change can be initiated, a pivotal event.

For some of my clients, these higher energies will manifest as 'the higher self', that eternal, spiritual part of our being. For others it will be as a guide or teacher, someone who is still on the 'human' evolution ladder, but who has the experience and the wisdom to take us further. You do not have to be in regression to experience these connections. It is perfectly possible during periods of ordinary consciousness. There are times, however, when a very special presence will make itself known. This presence takes on different guises according to the mind set and beliefs of the person witnessing the event. But it is characterised by a certain lightness of being, by joy and loving acceptance. I have come to recognise the presence as an Angelic being.

This is not a new phenomenon; there are accounts back into antiquity of encounters with the Angelic realms. The Bible, both Old and New Testaments, is, of course, full of such encounters. They are a feature of the religious life. One of my favourite Angelic interventions is described by the Venerable Bede, a seventh-century ecclesiastic who chronicled the spiritual history of the English nation. To the Bede, Angels and devils were a matter of fact, not of belief. He recounts how 'one among the Northumbrians, who rose from the dead, related the things which he had seen, some exciting terror and others delight'. The man, having died and left his body, was taken on a tour of the afterlife by a being with a 'shining countenance and a bright garment'. Having shown him the torments of Hell that await the wicked, this Angelic being led him to a place of 'beautiful light, and therein heard sweet voices of persons singing, and [a] wonderful fragrancy proceeded from that place'. However, entry was denied to him and his Angelic guide led him back to his body once again. He spent the rest of his life rigorously preparing for the heavenly joys to come. Not everyone has such a dramatic intervention by an Angel, but those who do invariably find their lives changed, irrevocably and — usually — for the better. I certainly did when I had my own near death experience and Angelic visitation nearly thirty years ago.

At that time, few people admitted to meeting Angels. Nowadays it is much more acceptable, but most people are still puzzled as to how to make contact with these celestial beings. A Company of Angels gives us a practical, down-to-earth introduction to these beautific spirits, spirits who turn out to have a sense of humour and who are fun to know — just the kind of people we need to enhance our lives.

In an astrological chart an Angelic presence makes itself known in the shape of unfolding 'Angel's wings'. The Angel's Wings formation indicates someone who has the potential to be very close to the Angelic realms, 'an Angel in the making'. David Lawson has this formation.

During the time that I have known David, he has
demonstrated to me that we all have the potential to be in
touch with the celestial realms — to be enfolded in Angelic
wings — to meet our guardian Angel not as an ethereal, other
worldly presence, but as a practical guide and helper,
someone to whom we can turn in times of trouble and of joy.
But it has also become clear to me that David has a unique
gift for contacting this realm and making it accessible to
everyone. David's clear and lucid guidance shows us how to
link to these realms for ourselves, how to invite the Angelic
forces into our everyday lives, and how to bring about a
spiritual partnership here on earth. His integrity and
authenticity mean that you can safely put yourself in his
hands and allow him to take you on a journey of discovery. He
is the perfect guide to the company of Angels.

Judy Hall
Author of *The Karmic Journey* (Penguin Arkana)
and *The Art of Psychic Protection* (Findhorn Press)

Foreword

You are an Angel,
Unfold your wings,
You were seeded from the stars,
And planted upon the earth,
So that you may remind others of their celestial origins.

You are an Angel,
Fallen but ready to rise again,
Tell the world what you know,
So that others may take their rightful place in the
heavens,
And in doing so,
Help you to fly once more.

You are an Angel,
Unfold your wings,
And fly upwards,
Into the loving arms of the divine,
For you were always loved,
And home awaits.

(Heard between dreaming and waking)

David Lawson, 1990

IN THE BEGINNING

There has always been an Angelic dimension to my life. As a child, lying awake in my bedroom through many a sleepless night, I used to watch swirls of energy moving around me through the darkness. Like many children I lived through periods of being frightened of the dark and of the monsters that I imagined lurking beneath my bed, but the patterns of swirling energy never frightened me; rather, they comforted me. They moved around my bedroom as if they were being circulated by air currents, shifting shape and direction, breaking up and reforming. They appeared to be softly illuminated against the darkness, lit from a source beyond my physical perception. They could be both calming and stimulating at the same time but never threatening. Although the nature and personality of these energy forms would change, they were always loving and accepting. Looking back at my childhood I think my Angels were simply watching over me and waiting ...

CORDOBA

Cordoba is full of Angels. Angels peer out at you from pictures in gift shop windows. From the shelves of these emporiums, Angel figurines made of plaster dance, sing or strum their harps at passers-by, their images caught in mid-flight. Some are left bare, some are 'gilded' with tarnished gold paint and some, sporting more elaborate paint jobs, positively revel in their multicoloured gaudiness. Perhaps it is not surprising that this city in Southern Spain is so alive with Angel imagery. Its architecture reflects a history steeped in the cultural and religious traditions of both the Islamic Moors and the Spanish Catholics who conquered them, driving them south towards the African continent. There is even an historic synagogue in the city that stands as a reminder of a once thriving Jewish community. All three of these religious and cultural traditions include references to Angels who guide and watch over the lives of mortal men and women.

It was in Cordoba I received the message that I would be teaching and writing about Angels. It was not the first time I had received this message, but it was certainly the strongest, and it had the desired effect of making sure that I paid attention. My partner Justin Carson and I were temporarily living in Southern Spain. We had decided to take a year away from our home in London so that we could travel freely, teach a little and, in my case, have some time clear of my normal distractions while writing my book about astrology and self-healing techniques, *Star Healing — Your Sun Sign, Your Health and Your Success*. We had rented a charming cottage near Orgiva, a town in Granada province, which we used as a base for my writing and our gentle exploration of the Andalusian countryside.

Much of my astrological book was written by hand as I sat in the Spanish sunshine and inhaled the scents of orange trees and jasmine that were carried to me by the mild winter breezes. When the breezes grew cooler, I would retreat into the house to transfer my text onto my portable computer. This period of my life was quite idyllic, for in many ways the environment was filled with the Angelic sensuality that always inhabits wild and peaceful places, but I was too obsessively focused upon completing my text to really notice. Once I have allowed myself to engage with it, the spirit of a book can become quite consuming.

After I had completed my manuscript, we decided to celebrate with a three-day trip to the one great Andalusian city we had not previously visited, Cordoba. We had already marvelled at the two other jewels of Southern Spain, Granada and Seville, and had a growing fascination with the mixture of Moorish and Christian architecture that is typical of this region. Setting out across country in our conspicuously British car through glorious Spanish countryside and along dubious Spanish roads, I was able to release my book to the publishing process. My mind clearer, I gained a new sense of freedom, a renewed spirit of adventure and I was able to listen more intently to the whispers of the Angels.

We arrived in the old city of Cordoba and parked our car near the famous mosque, with its interior converted into a Christian cathedral, so that we could take our first look around at the architecture and locate our hotel at the same time. Without planning to do so we had inadvertently parked under a statue of the Archangel Raphael, who cast his protection over the area. As a healer and a frequent traveller I felt greatly inspired by the idea that Raphael was watching over me during my time in this city, for the literal translation of his Hebraic name is 'God Heals' and Christian tradition has depicted him as a patron of travellers. So parking in this auspicious location set my mood for the exploration that was to follow. Certainly our car remained entirely safe for the whole period of the trip despite the warnings of car theft in our guide book and the abundant evidence of broken glass from other car windows in the surrounding streets.

Our hotel was one of the smarter hotels in the centre of the old city. Inside it had a kind of faded, decaying charm and it was moderately uncomfortable in a way that old hotels sometimes are. It was greatly in need of refurbishment but had an air of unpretentious contentment that only comes when a place has been well lived in. Checking in and depositing our luggage in our room, Justin and I then returned to the historic streets to continue our Angel odyssey. We were highly amused by the number of Angelic images that leapt out at us from the architecture and peeped at us from shop windows. Angel spotting became an ongoing game that punctuated our walks around winding passageways and our meals in stone courtyard restaurants.

On our second night in Cordoba we had gone to bed at about midnight and I had quickly passed into a sound sleep. Suddenly, I awoke and found that my mind was filled with creative ideas and impulses. I did not know what time it was, but I knew that I was unlikely to return to sleep immediately. I was infused with a feeling of relaxation, comfort and well-being, but the creative power of my mind was too strongly stimulated to allow me to drift off again.

Before opening my eyes I noticed that my head was surrounded with shimmering lights. This did not surprise me as an internal vision of light had already become a common enough occurrence for me, particularly at night-time. Indeed, in the years that have followed, this vision of light has continued to increase. I knew then that when I opened my eyes the room would be in darkness and that the light would not be coming from an obvious physical source, so I paused for a few moments to enjoy the brilliance before allowing my eyelids to flick open and easing myself out of bed.

Dressing quietly, I picked up my writing pad and a pen and I crept out of the darkened room and into the electric glow of the corridor beyond. Like many hotel corridors there was very little to support me in my nocturnal creativity except for a battered armchair and a carpeted floor, but I took up my place in the armchair and began to write. I was facing the doors of the elevators and I was only once disturbed by a hotel porter who stepped out of the nearest one with an armful of newspapers which he placed outside the rooms for the occupants to discover in the daylight. He looked particularly startled to see me sitting there in the corridor in the middle of the night but greeted me politely with a mixture of Spanish and English before continuing with his task.

My creativity readily flowed from my mind to my pen and onto the paper. I could barely move my hand fast enough to translate my many nuances of thought from fleeting mental impulse to the solidity of the written word. By the time that I returned wearily to my bed I had written down some quite detailed ideas for a number of creative projects, including three books about Angels. What is more, I had a strong feeling that I had been charged with the task of helping people awaken to the Angelic presence that lies dormant within us all. As I lay on my mattress and the lights guided me back to sleep, I truly understood that all human beings are Angels in embryo, and I woke up the next morning filled with a new sense of excitement. A year later, on a short return to Southern Spain, I wrote a basic plan for the course that was to become A *Company of Angels*.

IN THE BEGINNING

As I begin to write this book, it would appear that the Angels are gathering to support me. In the last twenty-four hours, four of the participants from my recent Angels courses have telephoned me. In every case, the calls have been from individuals I have not spoken to for at least three months. I can also feel Angelic forces gathering in the ether around me. I am in the presence of guides and messengers eager to help with the task ahead. Despite this support I am finding that my initial resistance to writing is stronger than it has ever been.

This is perhaps the simplest and the most challenging book I have ever chosen to write. There is nothing complicated about Angels. Their purity of purpose is so brilliant that it is profoundly simple. It is just that the brightness of Angelic wisdom tends to highlight my human complications and challenges me to come to terms with myself. I cannot write without being as emotionally and spiritually truthful as I can be, and I am just not sure that I am up to the task. I find myself dodging and sidestepping, but no matter how hard I wriggle this book just refuses to let me go. So here it is. Please be kind to my mistakes and join me in A *Company of Angels* ...

Introduction
How to Use this Book

YOUR BRIDGES TO THE ANGELIC REALMS

A Company of Angels is filled with positive affirmations, invocations, meditations, visualisations and practical exercises to help you train yourself to be available for Angelic guidance, intervention and support. All of these techniques are simple to use and yet they are also powerful because they help you to focus the resources of your mind upon your desired goals. They are designed to stimulate your imagination, help modify your attitudinal state and clarify your intention so that the Angels can work with you in a way that is both appropriate to your needs and in tune with the essential nature of Angelic intervention. This is a little like tuning a radio to a particular frequency so that you can get the clearest reception with the best sound quality and so derive the greatest enjoyment from your favourite music show.

While the techniques suggested are specially written for the purpose of connecting you with your Angels, please feel free to adapt them for your own comfort. No person has the same kind of mind or imagination as another. Despite our similarities, our minds are individually creative; we each have our own unique style of thinking, learning and communicating. It is your intention and desire to connect with the Angels that is most important for success. To help you I have created the following simple guide to the use of positive thought techniques. For those readers who wish to explore the power of positive thought in greater depth, I have provided more information in my books *Principles of Self-healing* and *I See Myself in Perfect Health — Your Essential Guide to Self-healing*.

THE USE OF AFFIRMATIONS AND INVOCATIONS

The use of positive thought techniques for health, personal development, spiritual growth and general well-being is not a new concept. Many people have been aware of the power of words and positive visual images for centuries. In recent times, successful self-help books have catered for a growing desire that many people have to learn more about the power of the mind and to become more aware of their inner strengths so that, through these techniques, they can transform their lives. Many complementary therapists have successfully utilised will-power and imagery alongside physical, herbal or auric healing skills, and indeed, some practitioners of standard allopathic medicine are also beginning to recognise the value of using positive thought to aid or accelerate healing. In the workplace, many businesses are increasingly training their staff to think for success, as positive thought techniques are linked with the teaching of communication skills and effective management styles.

Within *A Company of Angels* I have included a series of positive affirmations and invocations for your use. These affirmations and invocations are bold, bright, positively focused statements or ideas that can be used to transform mental attitudes, attract Angelic guidance and aid mental, emotional or spiritual healing. An affirmation is simply a tool that can retrain the mind to think in more positive, constructive and life-enhancing ways. An invocation is a declaration or prayer that has the power to call certain energies or entities towards us. A positive statement of Angelic intent may act as both an affirmation and an invocation. It may both retrain the mind to be available for Angelic support and attract the intervention of our guiding

Angels. Either way, if used regularly, it will help to strengthen your connection to the realms of the Angels.

The thoughts, beliefs and attitudes that we hold directly affect the experience we have of our lives. Positive, joyous thoughts are much more likely to create positive, joyful experiences than negative thoughts are. Negative, limiting or rigidly held beliefs can adversely affect our emotional state, our ability to create fulfilling relationships and even our physical health. Many people are aware of the concept of the self-fulfilling prophecy and the idea that our thoughts affect our life experiences and feelings. Our minds are powerful. What we think affects the way we feel about ourselves today and forms the reality of tomorrow. We are more likely to be happy, healthy and prosperous if we are willing to believe that these positive experiences are available to us. Similarly we are better able to attract Angelic support if we take the time to invoke our guardian Angels and we can best utilise that support if we retrain our belief system to be available for Angelic intervention.

Using positive affirmations and invocations on a regular basis can help us to support the spiritual practices, career goals, relationships, exercise programmes, healthy diets and therapies that we have chosen, with brightness and love. What is more, the rhythms and discipline of positivity can help us to deal with and transcend the challenges of life, and to extend the bliss and pleasure of the good times. Affirmations and invocations are simple to use. They will work for anybody who is willing to experiment with them and who is willing to persist with their use when little or nothing appears to be happening. As a teacher of positive thought, I have observed that these are the times when the greatest breakthroughs often occur.

Most people would imagine that they think quite positively for much of the time, but there can be areas of old, restrictive or fearful thought that are deeply held or unconscious. These thoughts are often learned, along with some positive ones, very early on in life. The beliefs, attitudes and moods of our parents, or parent figures, were colouring our view of the world from day one. As we grew up, we were also influenced by the beliefs and behaviour of relatives, teachers and other children. Wider patterns of belief would have come to us from our religion, our community and even through the television set or the radio. Affirmations and invocations are used to replace old learned patterns of thought that no longer serve us, with new positive ones that do. By affirming positively, we alter our beliefs to support our needs and desires, changing our reality accordingly.

APPLYING AFFIRMATIONS AND INVOCATIONS

A Company of Angels contains many positive affirmations and invocations that have been specially created for regular use by anyone who wishes to enlist the support and guidance of the Angels. There are many ways to use affirmations and invocations. Here are some guidelines and suggestions.

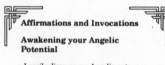

Affirmations and Invocations

Awakening your Angelic Potential

- I easily discover my Angelic nature.
- I accept my humanity and embrace my Angelic potential.
- I love myself and accept the love of the Angels.
- I ask that I be filled with the light of the Angels.
- My Angelic purpose now guides me to my greatest joy and highest potential.
- I am an Angel; I am guided by the Angels.

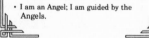

Example

Positive affirmations and invocations can be written, typed, spoken aloud, sung, chanted or said to yourself in the mirror as well as being repeated over and over in your mind. Many people find that they benefit from filling their homes with affirmational thoughts, perhaps writing or painting them out in bright colours and pasting them on the bathroom mirror, on the 'fridge', on the doors or anywhere else where they will be constantly visible. Be creative and choose ways to use them that work best for you.

Affirmations and invocations are wonderful when they are used in conjunction with meditation or physical exercise. Choosing one or two affirmations that are easy to remember and repeating them silently to yourself with the rhythm of your breath or in time to the repetition of a familiar exercise can help them to become second nature. You may even repeat affirmations or invocations in your mind as you walk, pacing them out with every step that you take.

Affirmations and invocations can easily be recorded for you to listen to while you are meditating, relaxing, having a bath, pottering around your home, travelling to work or at any other time you choose. You could make a tape by getting a trusted friend or family member to speak your chosen series of positive thoughts into a tape recorder. Ask them to include your name from time to time so that it is as personally tailored as possible. Even more powerful would be a recording of your own voice speaking the affirmations and invocations; again put your own name into some of the positive statements. For example, 'I, David, am passionate about my ideas', or 'Susan, you are always motivated by Angelic guidance'. You may choose to build up a collection of tapes to use over and over again.

Although it is wonderful to set aside some special time every day, or every couple of days, to focus on your affirmations and invocations, you do not have to view them as yet another task to fit into your busy schedule. The best way to use them is to make them an integral part of your life. You could affirm on your way to and from work, while you are cooking the dinner, while you are doing the housework or going through your morning routine. Perhaps the best time for you to do affirmations are those last few minutes at night just before you go to sleep and those first few minutes in the morning when you are still waking up. These are times when your mind is receptive and when you can influence your night's rest or the mood of your day ahead. After a time you may wake up with the positive thoughts already there in your mind, repeating themselves with brightness and clarity to welcome you to the day.

Some of the best affirmations to use are those that run contrary to your current beliefs or differ greatly from what is presently real and true for you. For example, if you are sick or unwell, it may seem strange to affirm 'I am always in perfect health'. However, it will probably be one of the most appropriate positive statements to practise. Of course, you do need to recognise what is happening to your body and make appropriate choices about treatments; while you are doing this, the exercise of affirming for health will support your healing process and help the treatments that you have chosen to work.

The more you use affirmations and invocations, the more they can work for you. Sometimes it is good to have a few favourite affirmations, or positive declarations, that you will always remember wherever you are, while frequently introducing your mind to new ones that address a particular need. You can never have too many positive thoughts, but when you are first introducing your mind to them, it is perhaps better to have a few that you will be able to memorise and use rather than an endless list that can be easily forgotten. Remember, affirmations and invocations are meant to be fun. Play with them, experiment with them and find ways to use them that are entertaining for you.

USING THE LONGER INVOCATIONS

In addition to the collections of short affirmations and invocations placed throughout the book, I have created a number of longer invocations at the end of each chapter. Rather than memorising and repeating these longer invocations, you just need to read them periodically, either to yourself or out loud. They can be used in conjunction with some of the other exercises such as the meditations, visualisations or written exercises that often precede them. You may, for example, read one through a couple of times before closing your eyes, meditating and listening for Angelic guidance.

===== INVOCATION =====

Welcoming Your Guardian Angels

I consciously invite my guardian Angels into my life.

I welcome my guardian Angels and thank them for their loving kindness and support.

I ask that my guardian Angels guide me towards my greatest happiness.

I ask that my guardian Angels guide me safely along my spiritual path.

May my guardian Angels be blessed as they bless me and may they evolve spiritually as they help me to evolve.

Example

CREATING YOUR OWN AFFIRMATIONS

After using the affirmations I have devised for Angelic intervention, you may wish to experiment with creating some of your own; here are my guidelines to help you:

- Affirmations often work best when they are relatively short and easy to remember.

- Affirmations need to be phrased in the present tense, for example, 'I now create ...' (present simple tense) or 'I am always ...' (present continuous tense). If you affirm for something as if it is already true for you, then your mind can more readily make the changes that will alter your experience of life. However, if you affirm that something is *going* to happen or that it *will* happen, then you are creating it in the future, and that is where it will stay, constantly out of reach. 'In three weeks I will be ...' will always stay three weeks away.

- In most cases affirmations need to be positively focused on your desired outcome, rather than on the situation or conditions that you want to release. For example 'I am healthy and relaxed' is a much more effective affirmation than 'I am never sick or tense'. The latter will keep your attention unduly focused on the negative outcome, continuing to make it a reality in your life.

- Your negative or limiting thoughts are the raw material for creating positive affirmations. Each negative thought contains the foundation for positive change and growth. 'My life will never change for the better' can become 'My life always changes for the better'.

USING THE POWER OF MEDITATION AND VISUALISATION

Visualisation is the use of mental images to create the experiences we choose to have in our lives. By using the power of our minds, we can daydream away stress, create calm and peace, prevent illness, promote good health, awaken our psychic or intuitive abilities, accelerate our spiritual development and strengthen our personal growth as well as build an effective psychic bridge between ourselves and our Angels. Many people have already discovered that the power of creative daydreams has a miraculous effect on their home environment, their career, their finances and their relationships. To change your world, you begin by changing the way you picture it; the rest follows naturally.

Visualisation and positive thought techniques work directly on the most important relationship of all — the relationship we have with ourselves. How else can we create health, love and success in our lives if we do not see ourselves as healthy, lovable and successful. While the term visualisation may suggest that the use of mental images is essential for the success of these techniques, it is important to note that many of us do not naturally think in pictures. If you are more comfortable imagining sounds, feelings or concepts than visual images, then adapt my exercises accordingly. You will be much more successful painting the pictures with words or creating a symphony of feelings than struggling to conjure up a purely visual image. The growing relationship you have with yourself can include a growing respect for your own individual learning style and mental strengths.

Within *A Company of Angels* I have created a number of meditations that utilise visualisation techniques. All of these meditations strengthen our connections to the Angels and sow seeds for the imagination. Some may help to awaken psychic or intuitive abilities; others are concerned with healing or personal evolution; all are intended to stimulate a new awareness of our essential Angelic nature. The use of visualisation is a powerful way of accessing innate abilities and providing keys to positive change.

> **• Invoking the Archangels**
>
> *Exercise*
>
> Allow your eyes to softly close and use your imagination to paint the picture, build the feeling or frame the concept of the following sequence. Imagine yourself to be standing in the centre of a pyramid of golden light. The pyramid has a square base with four sides and four corners that are connected to a single central pinnacle at the top. There is plenty of space for you to move within your pyramid of light and the golden energy fills you with a feeling of warmth and well-being.   **Exercise •**
>
> *End*

Example

SETTING THE SCENE

For all the meditations or visualisation exercises included in *A Company of Angels* the ideal environment would be a safe, quiet place that is warm and comfortable. Minimise possible distractions by unplugging telephones and ensuring that other people will not disturb you. You can use music in the background if it helps you to relax, but make sure that it is calming and melodic and without lyrics that would fight for your attention.

Lie down on your back in a comfortable position or sit with your back properly supported, making sure that your feet are firmly planted on the floor. It is preferable to keep your arms and legs, hands and feet uncrossed, ensuring that your body is open and receptive. Remember to breathe deeply and slowly throughout your visualisation and make sure that your body will be warm as you relax.

Once you are familiar with the images and techniques suggested within this book, you may wish to practise meditating in many different situations — sitting on a bus, for instance — but the scenario described above is the easiest. However, remember that these techniques are not to be used while driving a car or in any other situation where you need all of your concentration.

It is not important to follow every detail of the visualisation exercises exactly. It would not be very relaxing for you to feel that you have to work hard to get all of the details correct and in the right order. Just read them through a couple of times to familiarise yourself with their essence before settling down and trusting your mind to take care of the images for you. If it helps, then make a tape recording of your own voice guiding you through the visualisations or alternatively, you could ask a trusted friend to talk you through them.

Giving your mind the freedom to play is more beneficial than trying hard to be absolutely accurate. Remember, the more you play with the visualisations in this book, the easier they become. Please feel free to adapt any of the images to your changing needs or special preferences; after a while you may find your imagination automatically extends and enhances them.

PEN AND PAPER EXERCISES

There are a few written exercises in this book that have been created to tap your imagination and stimulate the Angelic potential of your mind. The key to the success of these exercises is to repeat them periodically and do your best to approach them playfully. If an exercise asks questions or invites responses from you, be spontaneous and do not edit your answers. A response that initially appears to be irrelevant or nonsensical could turn out to be the key to some powerful Angelic guidance or inspiration. If you are not comfortable with writing, you could easily do these exercises verbally with a friend noting your responses or you could record them on an audio tape.

However you choose to participate, have a wonderful time becoming joined with *A Company of Angels*.

Chapter One
Welcome to the Angelic Realms

Angels with dirty faces wear Angel cake smiles,
Dress in Angel fish colours and by you are
beguiled,

Two footsteps before you, One hand on your head,
Clearing your pathway is where Angels will tread,

Angels with dirty faces talk to you in your sleep,
Whisper sweet wisdoms, your safety to keep.

Angel Islington, 1987

GUARDIANS OF LIGHT

Many people believe that they have a guardian Angel who
watches over them, helping them to make appropriate
choices about their lives and keeping them from harm
whenever possible. Personally I do not believe that we have a
single guardian Angel, rather I believe we each have a whole
collection of Angelic guardians. I think we have an extensive
support team of Angels that have contracted to work with us
on some aspect of our personal and spiritual development.
The Angel often recognised as our guardian is usually one of
a smaller group of guides that have the most obvious contact
with us, acting as an interpreter or voice for many of the
others and bringing us reassurance when we most need it.

Some guardian Angels are only actively involved in our lives for short periods of time before receding into the background to quietly observe our progress or moving on to fresh challenges of their own, while others provide a more constant presence, giving us an ongoing sense of stability and continuity. Some Angels give their attention to our underlying spiritual growth, while others may support us to achieve the more worldly expressions of our spiritual development such as aspects of our career and material success. Any activity that we engage in can be a focus of our spiritual evolution if we allow it to be.

So what are Angels and why are they so interested in us? Surely evolved beings would have much more stimulating things to do with their time than become intimately involved with our human lives, dramas and spiritual development? We can only form theories about this based upon the subjective experiences of people who lived and died before us and upon our own experiences of the Angelic intervention into our lives.

Angels are spiritual beings existing in the higher dimensions, who influence and interact with the physical world in which we live.

I believe that Angels are a combination of spiritual, psychological and energetic factors. Angels are spiritual beings in that they exist in dimensions beyond the physical realm we appear to be inhabiting. They have methods of creating a bridge between their reality and ours; perhaps the greatest bridge is the one that links to the higher mind, or higher psychology, of human beings. They appear to be manifestations of higher, brighter forms of energy, which travel throughout the universe and which can be expressed through physical matter. This, I believe, is why Angels are often described as beings of light and why they can channel wisdom, support and guidance through human beings.

There are many examples of human beings becoming Angelic in their behaviour, presence and essential nature. This can be true of us all whether or not we have a belief in

Angels and whether or not we are recognised as being divinely spiritual by other people. Certainly charismatic spiritual teachers display Angelic qualities when they are working with groups of people, even if they appear to be far from Angelic in the behaviour that they display in their private lives. So called, 'ordinary' people like you or me are equally capable of being vehicles for Angelic energy, love, wisdom and awareness. Angels do not require us to be perfect or even for us to hold particular spiritual beliefs. They just require us to be willing to love, to evolve spiritually and to be mentally available for support.

Angels offer us love and support but they do not
judge us.

Angels do not appear to be concerned with class, race, income brackets or forms of 'holier than thou' spiritual snobbery. They are equally inclined to work with rich and poor, black and white (and every other shade, tone and colour of skin), female and male, heterosexual and homosexual, religious and atheistic. We are all ordinary and we are all special. Being human makes us as equal as the grains of sand that make up the most beautiful tropical beach and as individually extraordinary as a sparkling jewel. I believe that Angels see us as special and lovable without the human judgements and criticisms that we apply to ourselves and to each other. Indeed, some past beliefs about Angels have included many human prejudices, but from my experience, I do not believe that Angels hold those kinds of judgements. The light does not just shine on the righteous, the chaste, the moral right wing, the moral left wing or any one particular section of society. Angelic light is too big for human small-mindedness and too bright to be concerned with the dense vibration of prejudice.

To answer questions like, 'Why are Angels interested in us?' and 'Why do Angels support and help us?', I think we need to look no further than our own loving behaviour. Why do loving parents do anything in their power to love, nurture and protect their children? Would a loving father not prevent his child from running out into the road and into the path of a fast-moving vehicle if he were physically able to? Would he not pick up that child and comfort her if she had fallen over and grazed her knee? Would a loving mother not sit by the bedside of her sick child if he were suffering from a potentially terminal illness? The role of a loving parent includes guidance, support, education, socialisation and protection. Parents and parent figures provide children with a model of how to live as well as a sense of their roots and origins. I believe that the role of Angels in our lives is quite similar to this.

Angels remind us of our spiritual origins and our spiritual potential.

I do not believe that Angels are our parents in a literal sense, but they do remind us of our spiritual origins. They give us a sense of who or what we were before we took on human form and they provide us with role models of what we can become. For Angels, there is a vested interest in our development that is similar to the vested interest that loving parents have in the lives of their children. People care for children because they themselves have something to learn from assuming the role of carer. Having a child, whether genetic or adopted, teaches us to love and provides us with a focus for the love we have within us and the love that is channelled through us from outside sources. It also gives us an infinite number of opportunities to stretch ourselves creatively and develop areas of awareness that we would not have been challenged to awaken otherwise.

It is true that we have genetic and biological reasons for having children and supporting them to adulthood. The biological impulse to perpetuate the species and pass on our own genetic coding has been a key factor in our evolutionary success, but I believe these impulses to be symptomatic of something greater. I would assert that the perpetuation of any species is a symptom of the fundamental creative impulse within all life to grow and develop spiritually. With Angels, I believe the creative impulse that exists for their spiritual growth also manifests as a desire to perpetuate. However, in the case of Angels it is not genetic coding that they wish to pass on but their own spiritual coding. They survive and grow by perpetuating and propagating Angelic awareness.

It has been suggested that Angels do not exist except as an expression of our desire to make the world appear to be a safer place than it really is. Some psychologists would argue that Angels are the invention of a mind that needs to believe in some benign outside force in order to feel secure — a sticking plaster for the soul, perhaps, or an adult version of the kind of imaginary friend that many of us create in childhood. Even if this were true, too many rational, well-balanced people throughout the ages have claimed to have benefited from Angelic intervention to use this as a reason to dismiss this phenomenon as being without value. Indeed, stories about Angels are fundamental to numerous spiritual and cultural traditions.

Working with Angels creates miraculous changes in our lives.

I believe that Angels are real. I also believe that Angelic awareness is both spiritual and psychological in nature, but perhaps my most important belief is that it does not matter whether you consider Angels to be an outside influence or a collection of qualities that exist within your own mind. Either way a conscious choice to work with Angels creates miraculous changes in our lives and accelerates all aspects of our personal development.

YOU ARE AN ANGEL

Many books have been written about Angels, some, light-hearted collections of pictures, stories and quotes and others, heavy spiritual or religious explorations of the Angelic realms. The former are essentially Angelic soundbites that provide daily inspiration for those of us fascinated with and charmed by Angels. The latter are attempts to rationalise and categorise areas of spiritual enquiry, which as human beings, we can only theorise about. For example, many spiritual scholars have attributed hierarchical structures to the Angelic realms, viewing the hosts of Angels as being part of a kind of management pyramid with Angelic minions at the bottom and a white-bearded God as Managing Director at the top. While some of these texts may contain words of wisdom or inspiration, in my opinion the idea that there is a hierarchy of Angelic forces seems to suggest more about our human judgements and perceptions than it does about the Angels themselves.

A Company of Angels is quite different from the books I have described. Its purpose is to help you access and work with Angelic influences in ways that will make a practical difference to your life. It is intended to help you make up your own mind about what you believe. (The ideas that I offer you are chiefly based upon my own subjective experience and opinion, no writer can pretend otherwise, but I hope that my ideas will help stimulate your own innate knowledge and wisdom so that you can decide for yourself.) Lastly, and most importantly, this book is designed to help you access and awaken your own Angelic nature so that you may truly live your life with the blessings of the Angels.

You have the potential to be Angelic.

All human beings have the potential to be Angelic. We each have Angelic qualities, gifts and motivations that just need to be recognised and expressed. We may express our Angelic nature through our creative work or we may express it through the love we give to others. The forms of expression are infinite, but they are always guided by the Angelic forces that are attracted to work with us and they exist as a natural extension of our unique spiritual purpose. In short, expressing our Angelic nature is part of our spiritual evolution.

To be Angelic does not mean that we have to strive for some abstract concept of moral perfection. Nor does it require us to torture ourselves with self-denial or tie ourselves up in knots by trying to be some kind of ethereal goody-two-shoes. For many of us the confused religious baggage of morals that we grew up with may have left us with the belief that we need to suppress most of our human feelings, needs and impulses in order to become spiritual. On the contrary, it is precisely by being ourselves, accepting ourselves fully and loving our humanity that we open ourselves up to our greatest spiritual evolution.

This does not mean that I am advocating an amoral lifestyle. I certainly believe in developing a moral code that we use as a foundation for our lives and that we teach to our children. Indeed, I think we all benefit from a moral code that exists as a natural extension of our core spiritual beliefs and values. It is just that so many religious and spiritual doctrines of the past have become entwined with fear, prejudice, rigid thinking and unrealistic expectations. It is not surprising that many people either reject spiritual teachings completely, losing the many benefits that those teachings might contain for them, or follow one doctrine so doggedly that they deny their own diversity and suppress some aspects of their humanity. However, when we look at the core values of many of the same religions, we find the loving acceptance that I believe to be essential to the spiritual evolution of us all. What is more, any moral code needs to be adaptable enough to be reinterpreted by each new generation. The morality that we teach our children needs to express some core values of free will, flexibility and individual choice.

Angels are beings of fire, passion and light.

The Angels of the Judæo-Christian and Islamic religions were rarely portrayed as tame or sugary sweet. Instead they were often seen to carry out their divine purpose with passion, magnificence and zeal. If we are to have access to the full guidance of the Angels and awaken to our true Angelic potential, I believe that we need to love ourselves for who and what we are. In doing so we can work with our passions, contradictions and desires to create some positive changes in the world around us. For when we love ourselves we are not fighting our own nature and it is easier for us to share our love with other people. Loving ourselves helps us to love others because we genuinely want to and not because we are trying to live up to a distorted moral code. The Angels are much bigger than any human perception of morality anyway. As human beings with Angelic potential, we too are bigger, brighter and more alive than we were ever taught that we could be.

To begin awakening your Angelic potential here are some positive thought techniques to mentally repeat to yourself on a regular basis. There are a number of Angelic affirmations

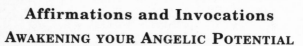

Affirmations and Invocations
AWAKENING YOUR ANGELIC POTENTIAL

- I easily discover my Angelic nature.

- I accept my humanity and embrace my Angelic potential.

- I love myself and accept the love of the Angels.

- I ask that I be filled with the light of the Angels.

- My Angelic purpose now guides me to my greatest joy and highest potential.

- I am an Angel; I am guided by the Angels.

- I have the ability to heal my soul and shine love into the world.

- It is safe for me to express my Angelic nature.

- I ask that I may recognise my own divine spark of Angelic potential.

- I ask that I may recognise the divinity within other people.

within this book. Their purpose is twofold: they will help you to retrain your mind to be available for Angelic guidance as well as acting as invocations to enlist the support of the Angels. There are also longer invocations at the end of each chapter. For a full explanation of how to work with positive thought techniques turn to the section on page 19 entitled 'How to Use this Book'.

ANGELS FROM THE REALMS OF GLORY

Most spiritual and religious teachings include a mythology of spiritual beings recognisable as Angelic. The minor deities of Hinduism may be defined as Angelic in character, as may the nature spirits of Greek mythology. However, many of our modern perceptions of Angels come from the teachings of Christianity, Judaism, Islam and Zoroastrianism.

The hierarchies of the Angels are reflected in the symbolism of astrology, numerology and divination.

As an astrologer and divination expert working therapeutically with a number of systems of divination, I am fascinated by the concept of the four throne bearers of Allah as described in Islamic texts. These four throne bearers top a hierarchy that is made up of Cherubim, Archangels and lesser Angels such as those considered to be guardian Angels. The throne bearers were symbolised by a man, a bull, an eagle and a lion; four symbols that also represent the four fixed signs of the Zodiac. The man is the astrological sign of Aquarius, the bull is the sign of Taurus and the lion is the sign of Leo. The eagle is an earlier symbol for the astrological sign that we now know as Scorpio, more latterly represented by the scorpion or snake. Indeed, many modern astrologers would still consider the eagle to symbolise the higher spiritual expression of Scorpio.

These four symbols of the man, the bull, the eagle and the lion turn up again in the Major Arcana of the Tarot. The last of the twenty-two cards that make up the Major Arcana is called 'The World'. It represents the completion of a spiritual cycle, journey, lesson or initiation and it depicts a dancing woman surrounded by these same four symbols. Within this context they may simply represent the four cardinal points of the earth: north, south, east and west, or they may be the embodiment of the four divine principles upon which the world is based. These four principles express themselves through the four seasons and the four elements as well as the four directions. In numerology the number four is an expression of divine order and structure.

Angels were imagined to be ranked in groups of four, seven or twelve.

Within Judæo-Christian, Islamic, Gnostic or Iranian teachings the numbers of celestial beings that were said to occupy a particular rank in the hierarchical structure described were often four, seven and twelve. These numbers have also been linked with the theories of Hellenistic and Iranian astrology and indeed, some texts attributed the rulership of the planetary spheres to particular Angels. For instance, the Sun was governed by Raphael, the Moon by Gabriel and Mercury by Michael. Some texts talk of there being seven Archangels in the hierarchy of the Angelic host, while others detail the four Archangels that we tend to think of in modern times. The first three I have already mentioned: Raphael, Gabriel and Michael; the fourth is known as Uriel.

THE FOUR ARCHANGELS

The Archangels were considered to be the rulers, or princes, of the Angels, each having special powers and areas of divine responsibility. While I consider it more important to access the Angelic influences that are available to us for our own individual development, I do think the four Archangels have valuable gifts to offer. As with the four throne bearers of Allah, the four fixed signs of the Zodiac, and the four cardinal points, I believe that the four Archangels are a representation of the four divine principles. These four principles may be described as spiritual laws that are reflected in the laws of nature. As above, so below.

Of course, the number four is not the only number to have powerful spiritual significance. For example, three is the number of the divine trinity that is central to Christian teachings, to the symbolism of Egyptian mythology and to many other religious traditions. The four Archangels are one expression of human attempts to explain the structure of the world we see around us and the universe in which this world exists as a microcosm. Invoking the four Archangels, either individually or together, is a powerful way of working in harmony with these divine laws. They can provide us with a structure for our Angelic exploration that is both stable and familiar. They exist as Angelic principles that have been recognised by the collective consciousness of humankind for thousands of years. Simply put, the four Archangels are a form of Angel symbology that has been effectively tried and tested.

THE ARCHANGEL GABRIEL

Gabriel is the Archangel who rules the North. In Hebrew his name simply means 'Man of God'. In both the Bible and the Koran he is depicted as God's messenger. Indeed, it is Gabriel who is said to have heralded the coming of John the Baptist and to have delivered the message to the Virgin Mary that she was to be the mother of God. His Islamic name is Jibril and he is attributed with revealing the Koran to Mohammed. In Gnostic teachings he was symbolised by an eagle or an ass. Gabriel is the Archangel to invoke for all matters of communication and mass media. In the 1950s Pope Pius XII declared him to be the patron of electronic communications, so I have no doubt that he has been kept busy during the latter half of the twentieth century, an age of television, telecommunications and information technology.

THE ARCHANGEL RAPHAEL

Raphael is the Archangel who rules the West. His name is
Hebraic and is literally translated to mean 'God Heals', which
indicates that he was considered to be an instrument for the
healing power of the divine. Indeed, in a popular Hebrew folk-
tale, the *Book of Tobit*, in the Old Testament Apocrypha,
Raphael was said to be an envoy of God who healed Tobit's
blindness. Christian tradition has depicted him as a patron of
travellers and in Gnostic teachings he was symbolised by a
lion or a snake. While he is an Angel of healing, he is also
considered to be a spiritual warrior who conquered demons
and ruled one of the seven planetary spheres.

THE ARCHANGEL MICHAEL

Michael is the Archangel who rules the East. In Hebrew his
name means 'He who is like God'. Prominent in Judaism,
Islam and Christianity, Michael is attributed with being the
warrior leader of the heavenly host in the battle against the
forces of evil. Judaic teachings depict him as the protector of
Israel and the keeper of the keys of heaven. Within Islam he
was thought to control the forces of nature and provide
mankind with both food and knowledge. He is said to be
assisted in this ministry by a thousand cherubim. In Gnostic
teachings Michael was symbolised by a lion. Christian
symbology often portrays him with a sword or with a scale
upon which he weighs the souls of the dead. This latter image
is similar to depictions of the ancient Egyptian god Anubis
who was thought to weigh the hearts of the deceased on a
scale in the Hall of Judgement. Michael is a judge, a high
priest and a 'militant guardian of the faithful'.

THE ARCHANGEL URIEL

Uriel is the Archangel who rules the South. His Hebrew
name is literally translated to mean 'Fire of God' and, indeed,
he is known as the Angel of fire, thunder and earthquakes.
Judaic mythology also associates him with the heat of the day

during the winter season. Uriel is often assumed to have less importance than the other three Archangels and this is perhaps because there are fewer references to him in Christian texts. My own belief is that he is the embodiment of Angelic forces that are more mysterious in nature than those embodied by the other three, but that he is no less powerful. In Gnostic teachings Uriel was symbolised by a bull or a snake.

• Invoking the Archangels

Exercise

Find a quiet, comfortable place to sit and relax. Make sure that you are not going to be disturbed for a while and take a few long, slow, deep breaths to settle yourself before you begin. Read through this exercise a couple of times to familiarise yourself with the key points before proceeding. Do not worry about getting every detail correct and in the sequence as written. It is more important for you to have the general sense of what you are doing and to approach this exercise with a positive intention to enlist the support of the Angels than to try too hard to get it right. Trust your imagination to create a representation of the four Archangels that is ideal for your needs and do not be discouraged if you do not receive a strong impression of them when you first practise this exercise. If necessary, just read through the details, breathe deeply and let your mind wander; the Angels will do the rest. (For a more comprehensive guide to using visualisation and meditation exercises turn to the section on page 19 entitled 'How to Use this Book'.)

Allow your eyes to softly close and use your imagination to paint the picture, build the feeling or frame the concept of the following sequence. Imagine yourself to be standing in the centre of a pyramid of golden light. The pyramid has a square base with four sides and four corners that are

Exercise continued

connected to a single central pinnacle at the top. There is plenty of space for you to move within your pyramid of light and the golden energy fills you with a feeling of warmth and well-being.

Invite the Archangel Gabriel to guard one of the four corners of your pyramid and imagine him appearing to you in a blaze of glory. Visualise or imagine him in any way that makes sense to you. You could picture him as a human figure — male, female or androgynous. You could see him as a classical Angel with snowy white wings and a golden halo or as an intense burst of bright light energy. You could visualise him as an eagle or imagine him as a feeling, a beautiful fragrance or a sound as bright and clear as a bell.

'Gabriel protect and guide me. Bless me with the powers of Angelic communication.'

Invite the Archangel Raphael to guard the second corner of your pyramid and imagine him appearing to you in a blaze of glory. Once again, visualise him in any way that makes sense to you. You could picture him as a human figure, or you could see him as a classical Angel with wings and a halo or as an intense burst of bright light energy. You could visualise him as a snake or imagine him as a feeling, a fragrance or a sound.

'Raphael protect and guide me. Bless me with the powers of Angelic healing.'

Invite the Archangel Michael to guard the third corner of your pyramid and imagine him appearing to you in a blaze of glory. You could picture him as a human figure with a sword of steel, or you could see him as a classical Angel holding a set of scales. You could visualise him as a lion, see him as a burst of light energy or imagine him as a feeling, a fragrance or a sound.

'Michael protect and guide me. Bless me with the powers of Angelic vision and discrimination.'

Invite the Archangel Uriel to guard the last of the four corners of your pyramid and imagine him appearing to you in a fiery blaze of glory. You could picture him as a glowing orb of spiritual fire, a human figure, a bright light or a winged Angel. You could see him as a bull or imagine him as a feeling, a fragrance or a sound.

'Uriel protect and guide me. Bless me with the powers of Angelic inspiration.'

Take your attention to the pinnacle of your pyramid and imagine it to have transformed into a star of white-gold energy that glows and pulses with infinite power. This star creates an effective bridge between your normal waking consciousness and your higher awareness. It allows you to safely access the higher guidance of the Angelic realms in every moment and to channel that higher guidance in way that makes a practical difference to your life.

'Angels open my mind and help me to take the practical steps necessary to transform my life for the better.'

In your mind, ask that the Archangels offer you safety and protection as you embark upon your exploration of the Angelic realms. Ask that they

Exercise continued help you to work with the guidance of your own guardian Angels and also ask them to keep you stable, balanced and grounded as you awaken to your own Angelic nature. Take a few moments to notice and enjoy any feelings or inspirations that come to you as you bathe in the protection of the Archangels before opening your eyes and gently bringing your attention back to your immediate environment.

Exercise • **End**

═══════ INVOCATION ═══════

Becoming Angel Blessed

Angels of love surround me and protect me as I grow towards the light.

Angels bless me in every moment of my life.

Bless my thoughts, feelings and choices.

Bless my mind, body, spirit and emotions.

Help me to awaken my Angelic potential and recognise my own Angelic nature.

Give me the passion, courage and joy to express my Angelic nature in everything I do.

May I always be available for Angelic inspiration and support.

May every breath I take be aligned to the breath of the divine.

I give thanks for my life and thanks for the blessings of the Angels.

Chapter Two
Contacting the Angels

I have come at the wish of my heart from the pool
of double fire, I have quenched it.

Homage to thee, Lord of Radiance, at the head of
the great house, within night and darkness.

I have come to thee, I am glorious, I am pure, my
two hands are behind thee; thy portion is with thy
ancestors.

Give thou to me my mouth that I may speak with
it. May I follow my heart at its season of fire and
night.

From *The Egyptian Book of the Dead*

GETTING IN TOUCH WITH YOUR ANGELS

The people who come on my courses or read my books, and
the many others I meet through my life, often express a
desire to make contact with their guardian Angels. In some
cases these same individuals imagine that making contact
with Angels is hard to achieve or they think that only a few
clever or privileged people are going to be able to do it. While
some people may be more naturally intuitive or psychically
open than others, I believe that each of us can make contact
with our Angels if we choose to.

We all have the ability to contact our guardian
Angels.

Contacting our Angels is simple for two reasons. First, our Angels have always been with us. They have always done their best to tend to our needs and they are constantly available to comfort and guide us. Secondly, they have a very strong desire to make contact with us, but they cannot intervene in our lives without our full permission. Contacting the Angels can be as simple as making the effort to pick up a telephone and dial the number of someone who has been sitting there waiting for your call. You just need the will and desire to do it.

THE LAWS OF ANGELIC INTERVENTION

Just as we talk of the laws of nature that govern day and night, guide the seasons and direct the currents of the oceans, there are natural spiritual laws that our Angels endeavour to work in harmony with. Doing otherwise is being like King Canute, who was so overwhelmed with his own sense of self-importance that he ordered the sea tides to retreat from the shore and in his obstinacy probably got very wet as the waves continued to advance towards him on their natural course. (While King Canute certainly existed, the story itself may be mythological or simply a metaphor for some other aspect of his life and campaigns, but it does illustrate the futility of resisting an inevitable force.)

The laws of Angelic intervention are in harmony
with our process of spiritual evolution.

When you begin to contact your Angels, it is important to know something of the laws of Angelic intervention. These are not human laws of guilt, blame, punishment and retribution. They are not laws that are based upon our fears or our need to defend ourselves and stand up for our rights. Instead they are higher laws that relate to our greater spiritual evolution. When we are aware of these laws, we are better able to work in harmony with our own spiritual nature and as a consequence, we become more aligned with our Angelic guardians. What is more, having some knowledge of Angelic intervention, we become better able to ask for what we need and more receptive to the help and support that is available to us. While I am sure that I will never stop learning about the laws of Angelic intervention, there are five key areas that provide me with a foundation for my ongoing exploration of all things Angelic.

1. Free Will and Personal Responsibility

Angels cannot and will not rob us of our autonomy. Instead, they are committed to helping us gain a high level of personal responsibility. While they may guide us towards a certain path, it is up to us to choose whether or not we follow it, how we follow it and what we do along the way. For example, a guardian Angel may encourage you to make a career change that would be advantageous for your overall spiritual development. You may experience a series of coincidences that include chance encounters with people who are already on that particular career path. You may feel moved to buy a magazine you would not normally read only to discover that it contains an article about the job or vocation that you are being called to. Once you have decided to find out more about this potential career, you may hear of the perfect course, at a price you can afford, that would allow you to retrain for the tasks ahead of you.

In all cases, these 'coincidental' occurrences are likely to be as a result of your guardian Angels working hand in hand with your higher mind to guide you onto the path that will be most advantageous for your personal evolution. Whether you choose that path, how long it takes you to make up your mind and how you allow that path to affect your life once you have embarked upon it is entirely up to you. Often there is more than one path that would offer us the opportunities for the happiness and personal development we seek. If we allow them to, our Angels will show us the options available to us and provide us with the support we need to make our decision, but they will never force us to choose and they will not choose for us.

Utilising our free will and exercising our power of choice is essential for our spiritual evolution.

If Angels took away your free will and robbed you of the right to choose for yourself, then they would be depriving you of your most potent spiritual lessons. Indeed, it is often the process of choosing that is more important to our spiritual evolution than the final decision we make. Angels will not do anything that runs contrary to our will or that is alien to our nature. Every action they take is in line with our consent, whether we grant that consent consciously or unconsciously. When we were small children, our parents may have made most of our decisions for us and they may have provided us with the boundaries and guidance needed for our security. However, if our parents continued to make most of our decisions as we grew up, we may never have learnt the confidence in our own judgement and abilities that is required for effective personal development. At the higher levels of human and spiritual awareness, I do not believe there is ever any reason for others to choose for us; whether we are six or sixty, we need to develop the spiritual maturity that only comes through exercising our power of choice, and our Angels are committed to supporting us with this.

Angels help us to make the transition from victim mentality to spiritual autonomy.

There are times when even the most proactive and autonomous people wish for the pressures of decision making to be taken away from them. It may sometimes appear to be very easy to sit back and let some benign outside force make a choice so that we do not have to. At its extreme, the desire for this to happen becomes the core of victim mentality, a state where we abdicate from our personal responsibility, give away our personal power to other people or our situation and look for someone to blame when everything goes wrong.

If we enlist the support of the Angels, they will help to relieve the pressure, most of which is often self-generated, and they will provide us with the love, guidance and protection we need, but they will not make the decisions for us. However, with Angelic guidance, exercising our right to choose can often be stimulating, liberating, transformational and fun. Angels delight in helping us to step out of the victim role, to take responsibility for our true needs and desires and, in doing so, to become the pilot of our own spiritual journey.

2. Ask and You Shall Receive

There are many times in our lives when we need help, and the support we require does not appear to be forthcoming. We may curse our luck or feel as if we are a victim of our circumstances and wonder, 'Why is this happening to me?' The truth is that our Angels are always doing their best to help us, but they cannot directly intervene unless we are available for their love and support. There are many factors that contribute to our availability for help, not least the issues of free will and individual choice, which I have already discussed, but perhaps the most significant factor is our ability and willingness to ask.

We need to learn to receive the help that we truly need and desire.

You may have observed that, within human relationships, when people are in need of assistance and others offer to help them, their response to that offer is crucial to the quality of help they receive. For example, if you saw a man struggling to carry some heavy bags of shopping and asked him if he needed your help, you would be best able to help him if he answered you quickly and in the affirmative. If he initially refused your help or was slow to respond, it would take much more effort and energy on your part to relieve him of his burden. If the man really did not want your help or felt so uncomfortable in receiving it that he felt obliged to refuse it when offered, then you might not choose to offer again. Some people are so well trained to resist the support that they genuinely need and, in many cases, actively desire that they make other people work ten times harder than is necessary in order to offer it to them. I would guess that most people have played out both the roles in this scenario at some time in their lives and that we could all benefit from learning to receive the help we need, as well as offering it to others.

In many situations the need to be met is a lot less obvious than helping someone to carry a heavy weight and often that need goes unnoticed unless the person requiring assistance is willing to ask for support. In numerous relationships people are so scared of being seen as vulnerable, incompetent or unable to cope that they struggle with overwhelming tasks on their own. This is often apparent in professional environments that are competitive and that lack a healthy spirit of teamwork from the boardroom downwards. Team members are often too scared to ask for each other's support in case they are viewed as unable to do their job or in the fear that an ambitious colleague will take over their responsibilities and erode their position. Unless we ask for help in our human relationships, we cannot learn from each other or build supportive partnerships – and the same is true in our relationships with our Angelic guardians.

Ask the Angels for their help on a daily basis.

If you need the help of the Angels then ask. An indication that you are available for their support is often all they are waiting for. Once you ask they know that they have your consent to intervene and they have a clearer picture of how they can best help you. The assistance of the Angels may not always come to you in the way that you expect, but it will come if you continue to ask and are willing to act upon any guidance you receive. When we ask the Angels for help, it is often interesting to note the many ways in which that help is channelled to us. It may come to us through another human being or through a feeling of loving warmth; it may arrive as a letter, a telephone call, words of wisdom that leap out from the pages of a book or as a flow of direct Angelic guidance that we feel compelled to act upon. Get into the habit of asking the Angels for help on a daily basis and regularly thank them for all of the help that you receive. Everyone likes to be thanked; it blesses them and encourages them to give their help again. Angels are no exception to this.

3. Forgive and Be Forgiven

I have taught forgiveness as part of my self-healing courses for many years and I am still doing my best to continue learning about forgiveness as part of my own personal development. Forgiveness is a greatly misunderstood area of human experience and spiritual evolution. Many of us think that we will never to be able to forgive the humiliations, neglect, betrayals and abuses that we have experienced at the hands of others, and yet I have met people who have forgiven the most extremely damaging violations of their humanity and have found a greater peace of mind because of it. Forgiveness connects us to the Angels because it helps us to dissolve some of our heaviest, most damaging patterns of thought, belief and behaviour. The laws of Angelic intervention include an awareness that no-one is beyond forgiveness. Whatever we do we can be free of our past mistakes with the grace of the Angels. Angels always forgive us and they wish us to be free of the patterns of resentment and guilt that we allow ourselves to become entrapped within when we are unwilling to be forgiving of ourselves or others.

Forgiveness heals all wounds and helps us to be more available for the forgiveness and loving acceptance of the Angels.

Perhaps one of the biggest misconceptions about forgiveness is that by forgiving we condone the destructive behaviour of other people and make ourselves available for even more hurt, embarrassment and abuse. We do not wish to give the other person the satisfaction of being forgiven and we do not want to be a doormat who invites others to walk all over us. Sometimes it may appear that it is our anger and resentment that is holding us together and we fear that if we let go of those feelings we will lose ourselves in an abyss of emotional confusion. Nothing could be further from the truth. Forgiveness is not about other people, instead it is concerned with healing our relationship with ourselves and strengthening our connection with the Angels.

When we exercise forgiveness, we release ourselves from old negative patterns and expectations and in doing so, make ourselves available for relationships and experiences that are healthier and happier. When we forgive someone, we do not have to let that person walk back into our lives, move into our home or have any form of future relationship with us unless we choose to allow this contact or unless there is some practical necessity. Indeed, we create a mental, emotional and spiritual state that enables us to reclaim our power.

Forgiveness can help build a new foundation of trust and communication between people but that is not its primary purpose.

If a separated couple need to see each other regularly to allow their children access to them both, then there may be some practical necessity for an ongoing relationship, but even in this situation it is often possible to minimise the contact and for one person to harness support, both human and Angelic, that would allow protection from the other. In many situations we do not have to continue a relationship in order to forgive the other person, unless that is what we choose to do. Sometimes forgiveness can help build up a new, firmer foundation of trust and create more effective communication between the parties involved, but that is not its primary purpose.

Forgiveness can dissolve the resentment and guilt that might otherwise eat away at us. By forgiving we help to raise the vibrations of our thoughts and feelings to a level that is in tune with the Angels. When we forgive we are easily forgiven, lifted upwards and touched by the breath of the divine. Like many others, a woman who came on one of my courses a few years ago experienced a clear demonstration of the power of forgiveness. This woman, we will call her Helen, had not seen or spoken with her mother for a number of years, not since the two of them had argued badly. Helen longed for contact with her mother and guessed that her mother probably felt the same, but both were too hurt and too proud to be the first to forgive the other. After completing a process of forgiveness with my partner Justin Carson and myself, Helen wrote a letter of forgiveness to her mother, asking that they meet and put their differences behind them. She hesitated before mailing this letter but told herself that she had nothing to lose and mailed it anyway. Immediately she felt lighter, happier and more peaceful than she had felt for a number of years.

Forgiveness can liberate us from stalemate and enhance our spiritual development.

The very next morning, Helen received a letter from her mother in the mail also expressing a willingness to forgive and wishing for contact. The two letters had crossed in the post! It was as if there had been some kind of telepathic communication between the two women that allowed them both to make a move at the same time. Helen did repair her relationship with her mother, although they acknowledged that they were not going to agree on everything, and with the stalemate broken she was free to move her life forward in other ways. The state of unforgiveness she had created with her mother no longer existed to inhibit her spiritual development. Forgiveness had allowed the Angels to intervene and she had liberated herself to place her attention on more positive things.

4. The Power of Positive Thinking

As far as I am concerned, positive thinking is a gift to the human race from the Angelic realms. Positive thoughts are part of a language of spiritual fire and light that, when used, can talk to the very atoms and molecules that we are made of, transforming them from the human to the Angelic. If I sound excessively enthusiastic, it is because as a teacher of positive thought I have experienced the joyful enthusiasm that positive thought can bring and witnessed many miracles in my own life and in the lives of others as a result of positive attitudinal changes. When we think positively we raise our consciousness closer to the level of the Angels.

*Our thinking can make us magnetic to a greater
degree of Angelic intervention.*

Energy follows thought. Our thoughts and beliefs make us magnetic to some experiences and not to others. When we think positively we become magnetic to a greater degree of Angelic intervention. This does not mean that we need to give ourselves a hard time every time we fall back into a pattern of negative thinking. Instead, it means that we need to forgive ourselves and gently encourage ourselves to think in more positive, constructive ways. Thoughts of difficulty can become thoughts of ease, self-criticism can become praise and rigid thinking can give way to mental flexibility.

The laws of Angelic intervention include the law of mental karma. The Angels willingly provide human beings with the support that is congruent with their thought patterns, beliefs, expectations and imagination. Simply put, the Angels can only give us the feelings, experiences, opportunities and gifts that our mental state will allow. When we think positively, exercise our positive future vision and allow ourselves to dream, then we give the Angels greater opportunity to bless us with our hearts' desires.

Affirmations and Invocations
ATTRACTING ANGELIC CONTACT

- I now invite Angels into my life.

- I ask for the help of the Angels and I gratefully receive it.

- I strengthen the bond between myself and my guardian Angels.

- I open my mind to the guidance of the Angels.

- I easily communicate with Angelic forces.

- My life is filled with Angels.

- I create a telepathic link between myself and the messengers of higher guidance.

- My imagination is a bridge to the realms of the Angels.

- I am willing to experience the presence of the Angels in my everyday life.

- My Angels fill me with Angelic inspiration.

5. Love Reigns Supreme

Even when we do not ask for the help and support of the Angels, they continue to love us. Our guardian Angels have always loved us and they always will; nothing we do, think or say will alter that. Angelic beings see humans as beautiful, special and unique. Each human soul is like a precious jewel among precious jewels. There may be many similarities from one to another, but there are no two that are exactly the same and all are divinely lovable. When we resist this divine law by not loving ourselves and by believing that we are unlovable, we are like King Canute ordering the waves to retreat. Whatever we do, we are still going to get wet, so we might as well learn to swim or at the very least, paddle. The times in our lives when we feel unloved are simply times when we do not allow ourselves to receive the love that is available for us. Angels do not give up on us even when we give up on ourselves.

Love connects us to the Angelic realms.

When we ourselves express love, ask for the love we need or learn to love ourselves a little better, then the contact we have with our Angels is strengthened. Love is a language that Angels understand well and can readily respond to. Taking our attention away from the things we fear, dread and hate and instead placing our attention upon what we love raises the vibration of our natural spiritual energy. Everything around us is made up of energy. Matter is energy, sound is energy and so is colour. All energy vibrates at a certain frequency, or vibrational rate. The matter that makes up the human body is a form of energy that is connected to a subtle field of electromagnetic resonance that is higher and finer than matter itself. The higher and faster we vibrate, the closer our electromagnetic resonance becomes to the resonance of the Angels. Simply put, the more we immerse ourselves in love, the more Angelic we become and the more available we are for Angelic intervention.

ATTRACTING ANGELS WITH LOVE

Just as Angels are attracted by light because they instinctively recognise their likeness within it and are magnetised by their likeness, Angels are always attracted by love. This is one of the reasons that Angels are powerfully drawn to young children. Unless and until they are taught otherwise, children express their love, like all their emotions, in a free, direct and uncomplicated manner. It is during childhood that many of us are at our most unconditionally loving, which is perhaps why Christian teaching places a strong emphasis upon the value of 'being as little children'.

My grandfather Ron died recently, he was eighty-six and blessed with having achieved a full and rich life. Although he had become steadily less capable of looking after himself during his final years, he had been looked after with grace, love and courage by my Nana Doris, a woman who, at eighty-five herself, has the most inspiring combination of sensitivity, good humour and cast-iron will that I have ever encountered. My Nana's determination ensured that my Grandpa was able to remain in his own home until just two days before he died.

The people, places and activities we love connect us with the realms of the Angels.

During Grandpa's last two days in hospital, I sensed that he was probably about to die and my mind was filled with a triumphant symphony of memories. I remembered my childhood experiences of him with his shock of crisp white hair, his ruddy, youthful face and his rounded figure. I also remembered details about him that had come to me indirectly in the form of family stories. Every family has its own special mythology of past events, misadventures and achievements, some spoken about freely and some not; my family is no exception.

My Grandpa Ron was one of the most creative people I have ever known. He described himself as 'a jack of all trades, master of none', but this was far from the truth. In reality he mastered most of the skills that he turned his attention to and was a brilliant engineer; a self-taught musician, who could play a number of musical instruments without ever having learned to read music; a clever craftsman with wood, metal and a number of other materials; a driving instructor; a card sharp and a natural entertainer – all this for a man who, as a school boy, had been placed bottom of the class below the one he was supposed to be in.

Our spirit is expressed through love, passion and celebration.

One overriding idea emblazoned itself on my mind as I thought about my Grandpa. In a flash I realised that the spirit of the man was contained within the creativity and love that he had expressed throughout his life. Indeed for all of us, our love, passion and creativity say more about us than words ever can. The things we love, enjoy and celebrate liberate our spirits to touch the divine. Love is truly the primary language of the Angels. My Grandfather loved his family. He also loved being the centre of attention and he loved to make people laugh. His spirit continues to shine in the world through the residue of his love.

It is often the things we love to do that most express our Angelic qualities. Two and a half years ago one of my closest friends died of cancer. Her name was Francesca Montaldi and she was a wonderfully eccentric, curious and friendly Italian woman who lived in London and worked as an acupuncturist. I associate her with the Angels because she turned some of her own life problems into the fuel for healing the problems of others and making a positive difference to the world in which she lived. When she treated her patients, she usually wore a white lab coat with an Angel brooch pinned to her lapel and she used to call my partner and me her two guardian Angels. When I first met Francesca, it was clear that she loved being an acupuncturist and, in the time I knew her, it was obvious that she treated each of her regular clients like the most precious person on earth.

Francesca loved to go to the cinema with her girlfriends or watch the latest episode of *Star Trek – The Next Generation* on the television, and some of my best memories of her are of going for a walk through one of a selection of north London parks, stopping enroute to buy some good quality Italian ice cream. This was a ritual she loved so much that she often could not contain her excitement as she encouraged her friends to accompany her. Amongst her many achievements, Francesca also founded a college of acupuncture, which she loved dearly. She particularly loved her first students, most of whom became fine practising acupuncturists, inspired greatly by her and her love for this brilliant form of ancient Chinese medicine.

When we place our attention on love and celebration
we make ourselves magnetic to the loving
intervention of the Angels.

For the living, placing our attention on the people and things we love or taking time to do what we love automatically makes us more available for Angelic intervention. Angels want us to be happy. They delight in our enjoyment and they are drawn to working with people who do their best to fill their lives with love. The more we place our attention on love and celebration, the easier it becomes for the Angels to fill our lives with loving people, exciting opportunities and feelings of spiritual fulfilment.

• Spinning a Web of Love

Exercise

Find a quiet, comfortable place to sit and make sure that you will not be disturbed for at least twenty minutes. You will need a pad of paper and a pen to record your instinctive responses to the following questions, but if you would prefer not to write, you could also do this exercise by speaking your responses directly into a tape recorder or Dictaphone.

Take a couple of minutes to breathe deeply, relax and imagine yourself surrounded by a radiance of bright golden light before answering the following questions:

What do you love and feel passionate about?

Whom do you love?

What do you most love to do?

Where do you most love to be?

What would you most love to do if you had the opportunity?

Exercise continued

How can you express more love in your life?

What can you do to receive more love in your life?

How can you best celebrate your life at this time?

How can you give yourself the most pleasure at this time?

What can you do to bring more love into the lives of other people?

What is the most loving thing you can do for yourself in the next week?

To complete this exercise, close your eyes and imagine the Angels spinning a web of love around you. You could visualise this as a web of gold and silver threads or simply imagine it as a radiance of loving feelings, warmer, softer and more comforting than a blanket. Repeat this exercise daily over the next two to three days and add more information as it comes to your mind. Take note of any insights you receive and do your best to act upon them. If there are practical things you can do to express or receive more love, then diarise those activities and do your best to follow through.

Exercise • End

YOUR GUARDIAN ANGELS

Being aware that the Angels can only intervene in our lives with our consent and that they can best operate through the vibrations of love, forgiveness and positive thought, we can begin to build channels of communication between ourselves and our special Angelic guardians. As I mentioned in Chapter One, I believe that we each have a host of guardian Angels looking after us, but we often communicate through a small number of guardians whose job is to provide us with sustained contact and be our bridge to the Angelic realms.

You will see, feel, hear and communicate with your
guardian Angels in ways that are unique to you
and your natural abilities.

Angels can present themselves to us in a number of different forms and they communicate in many ways. The way that you see, feel or hear your guardian Angels is likely to be congruent with your specific belief system and the way you most naturally receive information. If you are quite a visual person who tends to build an inner picture as a way of processing incoming information, then you may well get images of Angels that you see with your mind's eye. If you are an auditory person who is good at languages or focused upon music and sounds, then you may tend to hear Angelic sounds and guidance in the form of ideas or words of wisdom. As with visual people, you are most likely to 'receive' this information internally as if it has just been placed amongst your thoughts. You may be a person who is more focused upon touch, gut feelings and the flow of emotions than upon the flow of images or ideas. If this is the case, then you may primarily experience your Angels as a collection of feelings and sensations such as a particularly warm glow of love or a tingling of excitement that moves through your body.

Angels may communicate with us during deep sleep, visit us within the dreams of light sleep or come to us during daydreams, visualisations and meditations. They may even come to us when we are fully conscious and engaged in some seemingly unrelated activity such as washing the dishes or travelling to our place of work. They may have many faces, many voices and numerous ways of offering their love and support. Sometimes they may act or speak through another human being who is physically best placed to offer us the guidance or help we seek.

Angels can communicate to us through other
human beings.

I have experienced this kind of Angelic intervention on a
number of occasions, both as the recipient of Angelic support
and as the channel for the guidance of others. At a workshop
I was leading in Ireland, I once spent part of my lunch break
giving additional support and information to a woman who
asked for my help. I listened to this woman for a while before
feeling moved to respond with advice that I do not think was
entirely my own. Some of the words and feelings that I
communicated to her seemed to come from beyond me.
Afterwards, this woman thanked me for my help and she told
me that my eyes had changed when I was speaking with her.
She told me that my eyes had become 'the eyes of Jesus'.
While I would not claim to speak for Christ or for any other
spiritual teacher or prophet, I can recognise that 'Jesus eyes'
would be a natural method of communication between the
Angels and a woman whose background and beliefs were
based upon Irish Catholicism.

Be assured that your Angels will always communicate
with you in ways that are safe and that are appropriate for
your needs. It is not the intention of the Angels to frighten
you, startle you or provide information for you in a form that
you cannot use. If traditional images of Angels with snowy
white wings best fit your belief system, then that is what you
are most likely to see; if not, then they will appear to you in
another form. What is certain is that they will always come
to you with grace, love and humour and they will never
encourage you to act in a way that is destructive to yourself,
another human being or any other living creature.

- **Attracting Your Guardian Angels**

Find a quiet, comfortable place to sit and relax.
Make sure that you are not going to be disturbed
and take a few long, slow, deep breaths to settle
yourself before you begin. Read through this
exercise a couple of times to familiarise yourself

Exercise continued

with the key points before proceeding. Allow your eyes to softly close and use your imagination to paint the picture, build the feeling or frame the concept of the following sequence:

Visualise yourself standing at the doorway of a beautiful tower. As you look up you see that the tower is so tall that the top is shrouded in mist, far from view. Knowing that you are safe and that you are guided and protected by the Angels, imagine yourself walking through the door and facing a spiral staircase leading upwards.

Within your imagination, take your first steps onto the spiral staircase and sense a wave of delicious feelings swirling towards you, touching you and urging you upwards. There are feelings of peace, joy, love and excitement that gently encourage you to climb. What is more, as you ascend you discover that there is a new sensation of lightness in your movements. Perhaps your sense of gravity has shifted or perhaps there is a current of energy that propels you onwards because you easily find yourself moving up three or four steps at a time for every one step forward you take.

Imagine the climb upwards becoming easier and easier and visualise yourself surrounded by a light that becomes brighter the higher you go. Ahead of you there are the strains of beautiful, high pitched music and a fragrance so exquisitely seductive that it draws you on. Soon you are at the top of the staircase, facing an open doorway that is filled with light. You step through the doorway and find yourself standing on a sturdy balcony. As your eyes adjust to the light you look for the source of that radiance and the delicious sounds and smells that accompany it.

From the balcony, picture yourself looking across an open space to a high mountain peak beyond.

Exercise continued

Although the mountain is partly shrouded in mist you can easily see thousands and thousands of white and golden lights, like a mass of glow-worms shimmering in the distance. These are your Angels, ready to support you in a multitude of ways. With your thoughts, declare that you are ready to have direct contact with some of your Angelic guardians and ask that they may come to you and bless you with their love and guidance.

Imagine a bridge materialising between your balcony and the mountain peak and see a number of Angels stepping onto it and making their way towards you. As they move forward you begin to make out the specific forms in which they present themselves. Some may appear as beings of pure light or energy, others may be human in form or take the shape of an animal or bird such as a butterfly, cat, dove, eagle or hummingbird. Some may take the form of a mythical creature such as a winged horse while others may present themselves to you as a sound, a feeling, a fragrance or a concept. The form that each of your guardian Angels uses to present themselves to you may say more about your belief system than it does about their true nature, but their loving essence will still touch you nevertheless.

Step onto the bridge so that you may approach the two or three Angels that are closest to you and take some time to get an impression of each one. What does your first Angel look like or feel like? Do they come with a sound or a fragrance? Does this Angel have a name by which you will know them? Ask this Angel what their purpose is and what they have come to help you with. Welcome this Angel into your life and thank them for the guidance and support that is offered. Listen for any insights or words of wisdom that this Angel has for you at this time.

Exercise continued

Repeat this process with a second Angel and perhaps a third, knowing that there are others behind them that you may communicate with on another occasion. When you have made all your observations for now and gleaned any insights that are offered to you, salute all your angels before stepping back onto the balcony and beginning your descent. As you make your way down the spiral staircase, be aware that you have strengthened your connection to your guardian Angels and feel their essence safely guiding you back to earth. An aspect of your guardian Angels remains with you at all times to love and support you. You can talk to your Angels in your dreams, prayers and meditations, and whenever you choose, you can return to the tower and step onto the bridge to explore more of your Angelic relationships.

Once you are standing outside the tower, imagine yourself placing your feet firmly onto the earth so that you can be completely grounded and make practical use of the Angelic support you are now receiving. Thank your guardian Angels for their love and gently open your eyes, taking a few moments to focus upon your immediate environment before beginning any other activity. While your impressions are still fresh in your mind you may wish to write down any ideas or insights you received.

Do not be concerned if you do not see, hear or feel anything tangible when you first begin to do this. It is enough that you have the intention to communicate with your guardian Angels for you to attract greater Angelic intervention into your life. With practice you will become more consciously aware of the many ways in which this occurs.

Exercise • End

INVOCATION

Welcoming Your Guardian Angels

I consciously invite my guardian Angels into my life.

I welcome my guardian Angels and thank them for their loving kindness and support.

I ask that my guardian Angels guide me towards my greatest happiness.

I ask that my guardian Angels guide me safely along my spiritual path.

May my guardian Angels be blessed as they bless me and may they evolve spiritually as they help me to evolve.

May I bathe in the light of my Angelic guardians as they nurture and inspire me with their love.

I acknowledge my guardians for watching over me throughout every moment of my life.

I ask that my guardian Angels continue to guide and support me wherever I go.

Chapter Three
Angel Magic and Miracles

Do I believe in miracles? Do I believe in you?

You are my miracle,
One that descends from the deepest silver used to
line clouds.

Magic flows between us on many threads of many
colours,
As I surrender to your Angelic beauty in human
form.

A wave splashes over me and it's you!
A flower opens its petals to reveal a secret in my
heart and it's you!

Never leave me, my miracle, my every cell cries out
for you,
And yet, if daylight came and you flew away,
Then I could live happy in the knowledge that
I have experienced the best that life can offer.

And in some distant place when my face is lined,
I can look back and say that I have truly loved,
That I have met an Angel and that I believe in
miracles.

David Lawson, 1988

LIVING WITH MIRACLES

How would you define a miracle? Would you say that a miracle is an act of Angelic intervention? *The Oxford English Dictionary* defines a miracle as 'A marvellous event occurring within human experience, which cannot have been brought about by human power or by the operation of any natural agency, and must therefore be ascribed to the special intervention of the deity or some supernatural being'. *The Oxford English Dictionary* goes on to say that '... a miracle is chiefly an act (e.g. healing) exhibiting control over the laws of nature, and serving as evidence that the agent is either divine or is specially favoured by God'. Parts of this definition I would agree with, but with the definition as a whole I feel compelled to fundamentally disagree. Miracles play a much bigger part in our daily lives than it would suggest.

When we view something as a miracle, we connect
with the pleasure and magic of its miraculous
nature.

If we are to concur wholeheartedly with this definition of a miracle, then we may also believe that if we can explain or measure an occurrence by scientific means, it cannot count as miraculous. Certainly, when we consider our collective history, we can see that events and occurrences that were considered to be miracles a relatively short time ago are now easily explained and as such they have lost their mystique. Fire was once considered to be a miraculous gift from the gods. Indeed, in Greek mythology, Prometheus was severely punished by Zeus for passing on the secret of fire to mankind, which he achieved by stealing a piece of fire from the 'wheel of the sun'. Now that we understand the nature of combustion, we take it for granted that fire is the visible effect of a physical chemical reaction between oxygen and other elements or substances. This is useful in allowing us to create the chemical reaction of fire at will, in numerous geographical and chemical environments, but it does have its drawbacks. Fire is no longer seen as a miracle and as a consequence, we have lost the pleasure and magic that can come from appreciating its miraculous nature.

My belief is that it is counter-productive to view miracles as being contrary to the laws of nature. What we understand about these natural laws is constantly expanding, but just because we can explain something physically does not mean that it is somehow disconnected from spirit. Every physical occurrence has its divine source, everything that happens in the world is a gift from God and all events are connected to the Angels. The more that we place our attention upon the miraculous nature of all things, the more magnetic we become to miracles both explicable and inexplicable. A beautiful smile is a miracle, as is a butterfly, a jumbo jet, a seemingly chance encounter with an old friend, a change of attitude or a vision of an Angel.

Miracles are a change of human consciousness touched by the divine.

I believe that miracles are both natural and supernatural, dramatic and subtle, large and small. They are part of the natural laws of the universe in which we live and are available for everyone. In addition to viewing a miracle as 'an act of Angelic or divine intervention', I would also like to define it as 'a change of human consciousness, touched by the divine'. I believe that miracles are always there. We are constantly touched by them. Indeed, I consider miracles to be an integral part of the world around us as well as the world within. With a change of attitude we can learn to see them more clearly and make ourselves magnetic to their influence in our lives.

Miracles are a question of perception and timing: there are millions of minor miracles that surround us every day, but the way we view the world, the way we look at ourselves and the unique sense of timing that we each have, all make a difference between those miracles passing by us unnoticed and those miracles having a powerful and positive impact upon our lives.

MIRACULOUS CHANGES OF CONSCIOUSNESS

How often have you heard that if you change your mind you can change your life? This concept, fundamental to numerous religious and magical practices throughout history, has become part of the bedrock of the modern personal development movement. It indicates that new choices can bring new results and a little knowledge can be a revolution. Indeed, I could add that rather than being dangerous, knowledge has the power to liberate and heal, but it is what we do with our knowledge that makes the difference. If we are mentally available for miracles, then the miracles that fill our lives can touch us in ways that are joyful, practical and life-changing. In addition, if we are willing to be moved by the miraculous and willing to notice miracles on a daily basis, then they will grow and multiply. Miraculous changes of consciousness may be inspired by the Angels, but it is what we choose to do within our own minds that can make us available for Angel magic. We have already discussed the power of positive thinking, but let us look at some other factors that are key to becoming mentally receptive to miracles, great and small.

DISCOVERING THE POWER OF CHOICE

When I teach courses in healing, self-healing and personal development, I am constantly reminded of the power of personal choice in my own life as well as in the lives of the people I come into contact with. Many of us did not learn enough about our ability to choose when we were growing up. Even people who have learned to be assertive or who have many skills that support their self-esteem often forget that they have the power of choice. We often accept things that occur in our lives because we assume they are unchangeable or simply because we do not imagine that we can choose to create a different experience of the life path that is unfolding before us. A choice is a miraculous change of consciousness, as is the realisation that we have the power to make a new choice when our previous choices no longer serve us.

*Angels help us to make new choices by sending us
'flashes of light'.*

Our Angels often encourage us to make new choices. Sometimes we receive ideas and impulses that are a revelation to us. On an emotional level we may be filled with the energy of a potent desire to do something that runs contrary to our current life path, situation or expectations. On a mental level this can be like someone switching on a light. The image of a cartoon character with a light-bulb appearing above her head is a clear illustration of this. These 'flashes of light' may motivate us to step aside from our well-trodden path and cut a new one that is more in line with our true nature. Many years ago I was engaged to be married to a young woman who was very special, kind and caring. She was highly sensitive and very intelligent with a great sense of humour and a big heart. She and I were good friends with similar interests and, at the time, similar career goals. We lived together for a few months and began to plan our wedding, but at some level I knew that this was not the right relationship for me. I had assumed that having made the choice to marry this girl I could not make a different choice and I was in denial of my true needs, feelings and aspirations.

One weekend I participated in a personal development course that focused upon unleashing and expressing the unique creativity of the people involved. The joyful, positive nature of the weekend allowed my Angels to touch me in ways that I had blocked for some time previously. My natural intuitive and psychic abilities became heightened and I received an expanded vision of my life goals, needs and future potential. This came to me as a bright, vivid series of images and feelings, a bit like a movie playing within my mind and body. I instantly knew that the life path I was choosing for myself was fundamentally wrong. I saw the bigger picture of my current relationship and knew that if I married my fiancé, we would both become unhappy, frustrated and bitter.

Within forty-eight hours I had told my girlfriend that I could not marry her and within a month we had separated entirely. The way that I did this may not have been particularly Angelic, as my then lack of maturity teamed with my emotional confusion clouded my behaviour, but it was still the right thing to do. My Angels helped me to look at myself, make some new choices about my life and stop myself making a mistake that would have been detrimental to both our lives. Nine months later I awoke one morning with the knowledge that the Angels had visited me in my sleep. They came to tell me that I was about to meet my true life partner. They were right. Within a few weeks we met and fell in love, but that is another story ...

With the grace of the Angels, everything can be changed.

Even things that cannot be changed on the outside can be changed within. The Angels do not wish us to be miserable; they do not want us to suffer with pain, guilt, fear and loss. When someone we love dies we cannot bring them back, but we do not have to die spiritually or give up on life because we are bereaved. How we choose to grieve, what we choose to do with our feelings of grief and the many new choices we make about ourselves can make an extraordinary difference to our personal growth. We need to come to terms with what has happened so that we can move on to the next phase of life rather than getting stuck in the past. What we can choose to change in this situation is the way that we think about it and the way we respond. The Angels bless us when we make new, constructive choices and they help us to move towards the new opportunities that can best contribute to our future happiness. Perhaps the most important choice we can make as we build our connections to the Angels is to view everything that happens to us as miraculous.

SHIFTING YOUR ATTENTION

Whatever we place our attention upon grows. This is another ancient magical truth that has been adopted by the modern personal development movement. The reason that we get stuck in negative patterns and keep ourselves disconnected

Affirmations and Invocations
THE MIRACULOUS POWER OF CHOICE

- I always make choices that are guided by the Angels.

- With the grace of the Angels, everything can change for the better.

- I choose the miracles of free will and positive action.

- I change my mind to change my destiny.

- I now experience miraculous changes of consciousness.

- It is easy for me to exercise the power of choice.

- I choose love, freedom and Angel wisdom.

- I choose to attract an abundance of Angelic miracles.

- My mind is filled with miracles.

- I choose to see miracles within every aspect of my life.

from our Angels is often because we unduly place our attention upon occurrences, feelings, beliefs and expectations that do not serve us. In my experience of counselling, healing and human development I have observed that the people who keep their attention upon solutions do far better than those who are fixed upon the problem. Similarly, those people who are willing to look for the gift that they receive from even the most challenging occurrences have a greater chance of receiving Angelic support than those who see these occurrences as a personal blight or curse. This does not mean that we pretend that everything is fine when it is not; it does not serve us to hide behind a mask of love and light when we are filled with pain, sadness, anger or grief. We need to have a good cry, acknowledge our situation and then firmly place our attention upon the miraculous nature of our life. To create a memorable formula we can simplify this to the following statement:

Touch the feeling, pause and breathe, then think miracles, joy and ease!

If you wish to have a life that is filled with miracles, it is essential that you pay attention to the miraculous nature that is within all things. This is why we need to count our blessings and give thanks for what we receive. In doing so we shift our attention onto the areas of our life that serve us, digest the miracle of our positive experiences and give them the energy to grow and multiply. If our life partner does not understand our emotional needs, we could easily focus our energy and attention upon the apparent tragedy of our situation by thinking about it all the time and constantly complaining to our friends that we are starved of the love and care we crave. This approach is unlikely to make us happy nor will it help us to improve our relationship or give us the strength to move on and create what we truly desire elsewhere. If instead, we place our attention upon the love, care and understanding that does exist in our lives, whether it comes from our friends, our families or our wider support network, and we ask the Angels to bless our emotional needs then we are much more likely to find what we seek.

The miracle of placing our attention upon the thoughts, feelings and experiences that best serve us can help us work with our strengths, be available for the love that others know how to give and communicate our needs more effectively so that we can build bridges of mutual understanding. If you focus your energy upon your frustrated needs, then that is what you will continue to manifest in your life, but if you place your attention upon love, you will become magnetic to love. The same principle applies to everything. Place your attention upon miracles and wherever you go, miracles will touch your heart and mind. Be positive, be as clear about your needs as you can be, ask the Angels for help and affirm that you are available for miracles, then all you have to do is surrender to the love and guidance of your Angelic guardians.

TAKING A BIGGER PICTURE

On two or three holidays abroad I have bought and travelled with some disposable panoramic cameras. These are cameras made of cardboard and plastic that allow the user to take a much wider photograph. This is wonderful when you want to take a group shot of a large number of people or when you wish to have a bigger view of a beautiful landscape. I have panoramic pictures of the Grand Canyon in Arizona, Sydney Harbour in Australia and of a number of other large-scale, dramatic vistas. Taking a panoramic picture can help us to see everything within its greater context and bring our memories to life in a way that enhances the more detailed images of standard-sized pictures. I love it!

You are bigger than you were taught to be!

I often feel that we look at our lives as if we are looking through the lens of a standard-sized camera. In doing so, we come up with a small picture of our current reality and future potential when we could be taking a panoramic view that gives us a greater perspective. As with my story about cancelling my marriage and following my true life path, the Angels can help us to see the bigger picture of our lives and future potential so that we can chart our course by our greater vision rather than by our limitations. The view we take of ourselves is often dictated by the beliefs, opinions and inhibitions of other people that we have internalised without question. When we take a more expanded look at ourselves, we instantly become liberated from the small-minded, negative, fearful thinking that we may have grown up with, even in family environments that were essentially positive, loving and encouraging.

When I begin to help people to heal their lives, I often hear them describe themselves and their future potential in very limiting ways. Even those of us who are used to positive thought techniques and who are generally optimistic about the future tend to define ourselves by our past restrictions and limitations. Often we define our lives by the limitations of our parents or our peers as well. We make the mistake of thinking that our life path is directed by our past experience and present fears rather than by our dreams and desires for the future. For example, just because we have created a series of disastrous relationships does not mean that we are destined for failure and loneliness. We can make new choices about ourselves that make us available for something quite different from this present moment onwards and we can see our life purpose as bigger than just a frustrated search for true love.

You are an Angel in the making.

When we see ourselves as the limitless, creative, spiritual beings that we truly are and acknowledge that we have a special and unique contribution to make to the world we live in, then we enter the realms of the miraculous. When we acknowledge that we are bigger, brighter and more creative than we were ever taught to be by our families, schools or religion, then we can raise the vibration of our energy upwards and take wing. The truth is that you are an Angel in the making. You are an Angel that is beginning to fly. Angels in flight always see the bigger picture of life stretched out ahead of them and they chart a course through the heavens accordingly.

DISILLUSIONMENT

Disillusionment is both one of the greatest curses of the late twentieth century and one of the greatest blessings. Losing the illusions of childhood, for example, can be a necessary part of growing up, but in seeing beyond the fairy tales we also risk losing our natural childlike connection to the real magic of the world we live in. In our quest to become serious adults we may divorce ourselves from our intuition, spontaneity, imagination and wider vision. By gaining knowledge we can sometimes lose our natural ability to trust ourselves and to simply 'know'. In an age of television, information technology, long-distance travel and marvellous scientific achievements, we take the risk of becoming cynical and hard to please. We have a feeling that we have seen it all, done it all and got the T-shirt, even when we are sixteen, and that is far from the truth. Cynicism is supposed to equate to realism, but I have yet to meet a cynical person who is truly realistic about his or her life or achievements and I have certainly not met someone whose cynicism makes him or her happy.

Disillusionment applied correctly can dissolve the illusions we have about ourselves that inhibit our joyful nature.

So why do I also describe disillusionment as being one of our greatest blessings? Used with awareness, disillusionment can give us some valuable gifts. It can break down and dissolve the negative and limiting beliefs that we hold about ourselves and free us up to rediscover some of the same areas of natural magic that we lost when we stepped away from our childhood. Just as some forms of disillusionment can cause us to lose our sense of wonder, other forms can help us to find it again or create it anew from a perspective of true maturity. It is wonder, spontaneity, intuition, imagination and vision that allows us to work with the blessings of the Angels.

On a regular basis, ask your Angels to help you dissolve your negative or limiting illusions about yourself and notice the miraculous changes that begin to happen to you. For example, you may be living with the illusion that you cannot be happy while you are fatter than you would like to be. On some level, you may have bought into the myth that only extremely thin people are attractive and you may blame your emotional problems upon the fact that you do not look like the computer-enhanced images of male or female models in magazines. You may even be living with the illusory belief that happiness is not available for you unless you starve yourself and punish your body with extreme exercise regimes. Only you can change your mind about this, but if you ask the Angels for their help, you will be supported in making some magical changes of consciousness. Happiness, love and peace of mind are available to all once we have become disillusioned with our learnt beliefs and self-imposed limitations.

IMAGINATION

How often are children told to stop imagining things? The adult response to childhood imagination can range from healthy indulgence to crushing disdain, but it takes a special understanding of human nature and spiritual potential to fully recognise and nurture the power of a child's imaginative thought. In many cases, imaginative children are badly misunderstood, criticised and accused of being unrealistic or deceitful. It is not surprising that many of us learn to mistrust our imagination and make it a poor relation to so called realism and logic. I was fortunate to come from a family that encouraged my creativity and saw value in my imagination, but even I suffered from the lack of awareness of other people, particularly adults, when I was growing up. I was teased for being a dreamy child and felt self-conscious about tendencies that have become my greatest strengths. Had I not been dreamy and imaginative I would not have become a successful author, healer and psychic who has been able to be productive within a number of different creative mediums.

Your imagination is your bridge to the realms of the miraculous.

Everything we create in our lives is first created in our imagination and then manifested physically. All of the greatest inventions of the twentieth century were first created as a dream, desire or vision in the mind of seemingly ordinary human beings. What made these people extraordinary was that they paid attention to their imagination and did their best to turn their dreams into a physical reality. In my opinion they were probably all guided and assisted by their Angels. The imagination is the strongest bridge to the realms of the miraculous that any of us have. Through our imagination our Angels can speak to us and offer us ideas or guidance in the form of pictures, words, feelings and concepts. In the case of a great invention I believe that the inventor is most likely to receive the initial impulse to create a new miracle from the Angels themselves.

Once the inventor has acted upon this impulse the Angels provide the additional support, guidance and facilitation required to turn this dream into a reality.

If you nurture and listen to your imagination, you will strengthen your communication with the Angels and open the floodgates for the miracles you desire. Imagine a miraculous change occurring to your life within the next three months. It may relate to your work, your love life, your family life, your prosperity, your personal development or your spiritual growth. The truth is that if you can imagine this change, then you can create it in some form, even if you need to adapt your vision to the tools or resources currently available to you. Whatever miracle you wish for, if you dream it — you can be it!

BECOMING MAGNETIC TO MIRACLES

Somebody once paid me a wonderful compliment. He said 'It isn't that you create miracles; it is just that miracles love you'. This was said with such love and directness that it took my breath away and although this person was someone I met briefly and have never seen again, the power of his words has remained with me. What is wonderful about this statement is that it is true, not just of me, but of everybody; miracles constantly surround us because they are an expression of the limitless love that the Angels have for each human soul. We do not create miracles we co-create them by changing our consciousness. If you are surrounded by millions of butterflies and you are willing to be still and peaceful, then you have every chance of having a number of them settle on you for a period of time. If, in addition, you do not struggle to hold onto these beautiful creatures and you allow them to fly off when they are ready, then you will maintain the stillness required for more to land and settle on your body. In the words of William Blake, 'He who kisses a joy as she flies, lives in eternity's sunrise'.

• Creating a Miracle Shopping List

Exercise

What are the miracles you would like to create in your life? Would you like to be happier, healthier or more prosperous? Would you like to be more psychically attuned or spiritually aware? Would you like to open the doors to some new creative opportunities or open your heart to receive more love? Here is your chance to write a miracle shopping list to help both you and your Angels focus upon the magical changes that are going to occur in your life and the practical steps needed to achieve your goals.

Take a piece of paper and a pen and write down a list of the miracles you now wish to create. Do not dismiss anything that comes to mind for being too big or too small. It is foolish to assume that big miracles are beyond us and we never know how profound the impact of a small miracle might be upon our happiness and well-being, so it is best to include them all.

Write down each item on your list prefixed with the words 'I now attract the miracle of ...'. For example, if you wish for the miracle of mental peace and harmony you may write it in the following way:

I now attract the miracle of mental peace and harmony

or you may say,

I now attract the miracle of a peaceful and harmonious mind.

Here are some more examples of the kind of miracles you could choose to have on your list:

Exercise continued

I now attract the miracle of better communication within my family.

I now attract the miracle of a substantial rise in financial income.

I now attract the miracle of new career opportunities opening up for me.

I now attract the miracle of a loving, harmonious, romantic relationship with a wonderful man / woman.

I now attract the miracle of a healthy back / chest / hip, etc.

I now attract the miracle of true happiness and contentment.

The examples I have given are quite general. When you create your list you may wish to be more specific about your needs, feelings and desires. Once you have written down everything you can think of, sit in front of a mirror, look at your reflection and slowly read each item from your list as a powerful declaration to yourself and your Angels. Do your best to look yourself in the eyes as you do this. Begin by looking down at your list, get as clear about the wording of each item as you can and then look up so that you can declare it directly to your mirror image. Notice any thoughts or feelings that come up for you as you do this and make a note of any insights you receive. If you feel moved to do anything practical to put any part of your miracle list into action, then make sure that you do it. Your Angels could be guiding you towards the steps you need to take to facilitate the realisation of your goals.

Exercise continued

Complete this exercise by repeating the positive affirmation:

• I am magnetic to miracles.

Continue to repeat this affirmation to yourself on a daily basis, listen for the guidance of your Angels and act upon any insights or inspirations you receive. Add new items to your miracle list on a regular basis, read it to yourself periodically and give thanks to your Angels for any progress you make, no matter how small it might appear at first. For greater effect you could link this exercise with the following visualisation.

Exercise • End

Exercise

• **Invoking the Miracle Bringers**

Find a quiet, comfortable place to sit and relax. Make sure that you are not going to be disturbed and take a few long, slow, deep breaths to settle yourself before you begin. Read through this exercise a couple of times to familiarise yourself with the key points before proceeding. Allow your eyes to softly close and use your imagination to paint the picture, build the feeling or frame the concept of the following sequence:

Visualise yourself sitting in a beautiful garden that is softly warmed by the golden light of the sun. Take a few moments to build the image, feeling or concept of this place before proceeding and make sure that you picture yourself in a spot that is perfectly comfortable and peaceful for you. Once you are settled, ask that you be surrounded by Angels bringing you miracles and imbuing you with the powers of the miraculous. In your mind, repeat to yourself:

Exercise continued

'I ask to be filled and surrounded by Angel magic.'

'I ask to be visited by the bringers of miracles.'

Imagine yourself surrounded by a number of Angels. Some may be the guardian Angels you have contacted previously while others may be miracle bringers that are magnetised to you to help with your current needs and challenges. Notice how they all look, sound and feel. Do they come with a particular fragrance or sensation? What do you feel in your body as they come close to you? Play with your imagination and use it as a bridge to your Angels. As always, it does not matter exactly what you visualise, hear or feel as long as you make the effort to ask for help and you have an intention to receive the Angelic support offered you.

Imagine some of the Angels placing wings or hands of light into your mind to help you make positive, miraculous changes of consciousness. Picture others touching your heart to miraculously brighten and transform your feelings. Yet more Angels place reassuring hands of light onto your body to give you the miracle of physical comfort while a further group sing directly to your soul to remind it of its miraculous nature. Visualise Angels bringing you miraculous gifts, some that may relate to your miracle list and some that may not. The gifts may be in the form of feelings, ideas, objects, opportunities, money, crystals, flowers, new talents, special abilities or any others that are relevant to you. Receive each gift with love and thanks, acknowledging the Angels for their generosity. Make a commitment to the miracle bringers that you will do you best to make the most of the miracles they bless you with and ask that they continue to work with you. Affirm to yourself:

• I am magnetic to miracles.

Exercise continued

Once you feel complete, gently open your eyes, taking a few moments to focus upon your immediate environment before beginning any other activity. While your impressions are still fresh in your mind you may wish to write down any ideas or insights you received.

Exercise • **End**

=========== INVOCATION ===========

Merging with the Miraculous

I ask that I become one with the miraculous nature of the universe.

I ask that I be blessed with the abundant miracles of the Angels.

May I bathe in the miraculous and receive the many gifts of the Angelic realms.

May my life become a divine expression of the miracles that fill the world.

I am available for transformational miracles in all areas of my life.

I thank my Angels for the miracles they bring me and I celebrate my ability to make miraculous changes of heart and mind.

I ask that I may be guided to help others create their own miracles.

I ask that I make a miraculous difference, wherever I go.

Chapter Four
Angels of Prosperity and Success

With the grace of the Angels,
The riches of heaven and earth will be yours,
The brightest jewel and the sweetest flower,
All are prosperous expressions of the divine,
All are priceless in equal measure,
And all have value and no value,
Except for the value you give them with your
human heart.

With the grace of the Angels,
And an intention to shine,
You are magnetic to the prosperity of life,
Expressed equally through a loving smile,
A golden handshake or a passionate embrace,
You task is simply to receive and be happy,
And help others to do the same.

David Lawson, 1998

YOU ARE A MAGNET FOR DIVINE PROSPERITY

What is the feeling you get when you smell the aroma of your favourite food prepared with love by someone who cares deeply for you? What is the feeling that comes to you when a friend compliments you on your looks, abilities or acts of kindness? What is the feeling that you have when your work is properly rewarded with an abundant financial bonus? What feeling is invoked in you by the sight of wild flowers, beautifully coloured or the sound of the music you most love reaching your ears in the most unexpected location? These are just a few of the infinite expressions of prosperity that are potentially available to you. The prosperity of the universe is always looking to bless you with abundance, so it is important for you to become aware of how able you are to receive those blessings. So, how does being blessed make you feel?

Resisting the flow of prosperity deprives both the giver and the recipient of a valuable spiritual exchange.

Some people have great difficulty in receiving compliments and then wonder why they have a hard time receiving the money, love and happiness they truly desire. Perhaps we all block our ability to receive the gift of a compliment from time to time. When friends tell you that you look wonderful, do you smile, listen to what they have to say and only when you have heard them fully, thank them for noticing? How often do you resist compliments by disagreeing with the people who wish to compliment you, quickly changing the subject or thanking them before they have finished speaking and qualifying what they have said. When associates thank us for our contribution or support, we may respond by saying something like, 'It was nothing.' or we may appear to respond quite positively while secretly thinking, 'If only they knew how clumsy and badly conceived my contribution really was'. Either way, we have effectively blocked the flow of love and prosperity that has been offered us and in doing so, we have deprived both ourselves and the other person of a valuable spiritual exchange that would have benefited all concerned.

The Angels wish us all to receive the love and prosperity that will nurture our souls and contribute to our physical comfort. There is no blessing in starvation, whether physical, emotional, mental or spiritual. Divine prosperity in all of its forms is always seeking you. Indeed, it takes a huge amount of energy to resist it. We may resist a compliment out of habit or we may limit the flow of money into our lives because we secretly do not believe that we deserve it or because we have never learnt how to handle money and are afraid of it. The specific reasons for blocking the flow of prosperity are individual to us, but there are some key factors involved that are common to most of us. Perhaps the most damaging is the basic human fear of lack, or the belief that there is not enough to go round.

The Angels exist in a realm of abundance and so do we.

The Angels do not exist in a realm of lack and neither do we. Indeed, I do not believe that Angels fully understand the desperation, poverty and greed that manifest as symptoms of the human fear of lack although they do their best to alleviate those symptoms on a daily basis. From an Angelic perspective, lack does not exist; it is a purely human myth that creates an imbalance within the physical world, but it does not have any bearing upon spiritual truth. Once a critical mass of the human race has evolved beyond this basic fear and belief in lack, there will be no shortage of love, money and material resources available to any of us. Fear of lack creates the need to tightly hold onto what we have and that tightness automatically blocks the flow of prosperity out of and into our lives. Fear of lack creates desperation and our desperate energy stops us from being able to receive what we truly need and desire. It is like putting up a shield that deflects prosperity away from us. It is up to each of us individually to evolve beyond our fear of lack. In doing so we help change the collective mind of humanity from poverty consciousness to prosperity consciousness. Change yourself and you change the world.

THERE IS NO SEPARATION BETWEEN SPIRIT AND MATTER

In our human perception of the world we like to categorise, compartmentalise and label what we see around us, what we think or feel inside ourselves or what we imagine to exist. This can often be quite valid. When we give something a name or a classification, it can make it easier for us to explain it, learn about it and work with it. For instance, we give names to our emotions. We can say that we feel joyful or angry, or we can say that we are grieving. Naming our emotions allows us to make reference to similar experiences we had in the past or tell other people what we are feeling so that they can behave appropriately. They may not know exactly how we are feeling, but at least they will have a general sense of what we are experiencing that is based upon their own emotional memories.

On another level, scientific thought delights in measuring, categorising and sorting information about the world around us so that we can develop new technologies, find cures for the many diseases that currently challenge us and gain a degree of mastery over the physical world. When we are familiar with the properties of various substances or forms of energy, we can then predict how that substance or energy will behave under certain conditions. In this way, for example, we can be sure that certain chemicals act as detergents that will lift dirt and grease from fabric and we can therefore be confident in using them in washing powder.

Our value judgements about money and prosperity
may enhance our experiences or limit them.

The ability of human beings to classify, measure and sort is one of our greatest gifts, but if used unwisely, can also be the source of our limitations. Our human tendency to name and categorise also extends into a huge vocabulary of value judgements based upon our past beliefs and assumptions. We often decide for ourselves that one experience is better than another or that one kind of person would make a better friend for us than another kind of person. A blessing that can also be a curse, value judgements can equally be used to create healthy preferences or dangerous prejudices. They can enhance our experiences or limit them and this is certainly true when we make value judgements about money or prosperity.

Do you have a value judgement that some things are spiritual and others are not? Here are some common beliefs that could be worth questioning:

'Money is not spiritual.'

'To be spiritual is to deny our physical needs.'

'I cannot be spiritual and sexual.'

'Some people are more evolved than other people.'

'Some people are on a spiritual path and others are not.'

'Spiritual people do not get angry.'

Many of us have learnt that there is a separation between the spiritual and the physical aspects of life. 'During the week I go to work to make the money to live but on the Sabbath I go to the church, synagogue or mosque to praise God.' We create categories of experiences we believe to be spiritual and those we believe to be purely of the physical world. Money, as a material form of prosperity, is often considered to be purely of the physical world and, as such, it has developed a mystique of being dirty, tawdry and even downright unholy. We make value judgements about money being a 'necessary evil' and somehow believe that what we do spiritually and what we do financially are unconnected and that our purely spiritual pursuits are more honourable than our efforts to create an income.

I believe that spirit is within everything and everyone. Every person is on a spiritual journey, regardless of whether or not he or she follows a particular set of religious or spiritual beliefs. We may have physical bodies, but our essential nature is spiritual and this is true for all aspects of the material world which we inhabit. We are both spiritual and physical: there is no separation unless we create it with our belief system. We all experience anger at some time in our lives and unless there is a medical or metaphysical reason otherwise, we all have sexual feelings, but these 'human' qualities are not separate from our spiritual nature. Indeed anger, sexual arousal, grief, joy, sadness and an infinite number of other feelings are an integral part of the spiritual experience we all share. For, in truth, we are all spiritual beings on a human path.

Money is a physical manifestation of the spiritual energy of prosperity.

Money is just one physical manifestation of the spiritual energy of prosperity. Every banknote or coin in your pocket, every cheque you write or credit card slip you sign is a physical expression of spiritual energy. Your financial balance as it currently exists within the computer system of your savings bank is also an expression of spiritual energy. Whether you are in credit or have slipped into 'the red', it is an emanation of spirit. To change your financial status it is important to look at how you work with the energy of prosperity, how you receive it, how you use it and how you pass it on. It is also important to recognise that money may be key to your essential spiritual purpose and that by expressing your spiritual purpose you are more likely to step into the flow of prosperity.

MONEY AND SPIRITUAL PURPOSE

Angelic prosperity comes from fulfilling your underlying spiritual purpose and ensuring that your purpose is connected to the ways in which you generate your financial income. There are some people who seem to be born moneymakers. It does not matter what they turn their attention to: they are able to make a buck out of it. In some ways it could be said that the process of making and handling money is part of their spiritual purpose. The learning they receive in manifesting their income will ultimately help them to develop their ability to manifest and work with energy on the higher spiritual levels. Their focus may change in their later years or perhaps, in their next life once their financial learning is complete.

Money may be inextricably linked to your spiritual
purpose in one, or more, of a number of ways.

For other people, the need to create a financial income to feed themselves and their family is the motivation they require to hone their skills and engage with the world around them. Making money is not their primary purpose, but the need to do so facilitates their achieving the things that will evolve them spiritually. For example, a man who works as a cab driver may not wish to work at all and would perhaps not do anything if he did not have to support his family. The need to bring in an income motivates him to drive five days a week and in doing so, he uses the skills of driving, navigation and customer care to help him develop. Indeed, he may get most of his spiritual learning from the relationships he forms with his fellow drivers, employers and clients. Once he has learnt everything he can from that particular job, he may move on to something else that requires different skills, but it is the basic need to bring home the dough that gives him the motivation to go out into the world on a regular basis.

For many, the spiritual purpose of making money is primarily so that they can provide for others. They may gain much of their spiritual learning from being a parent and providing the material and emotional security for their children to thrive, grow and develop their own spiritual potential. A single mother may hold down two jobs and still be available to wipe noses, read bedtime stories, cuddle, teach and love. This is a huge amount for any one person to handle alone (it is amazing how many people do it), but it is achieved because of the necessity of the situation and because, in a number of cases, there is a basic spiritual purpose that is fulfilled in the act of providing. By giving to our children we give ourselves some extraordinary spiritual learning.

Money may not always be a key factor in our spiritual
purpose, but it always impinges upon our lives.

There are some people for whom money is not a key factor in their spiritual purpose. This does not mean that money does not impinge upon their life purpose in any way. No one can be part of a society that is run on a financial exchange system and not be affected by it, but some may be emotionally and spiritually liberated from the overriding need that many of us have to manifest an income. These may include the very rich who were born into money, those who have their money provided and managed for them by a partner and those who have a relatively modest income but who also have very few material desires.

Perhaps you can relate to one or more of these examples, or perhaps you simply make money to pay for the experiences you desire to create. Regardless of the specific relationship between the money in your life and your spiritual purpose, you can enlist the support of the Angels to enhance your prosperity. Prosperity is much more than just the flow of money into and out of our lives, but this does not mean we can negate money as being some lesser form of spiritual energy and learn to live directly on Angel dust and sunshine. Money is the most tangible form of prosperity that we exchange and operate with in contemporary society. The abundance or lack of it can say a great deal about the overall flow of prosperity. Our ability to make, work with, manage and enjoy our money is usually symptomatic of other things in our lives, such as our basic survival impulses, our quest for freedom and our ability to give and receive love.

Angels will assist with the flow of prosperity to facilitate your spiritual growth.

Money is neither good nor evil. Money is simply a form of energy we use to exchange with each other, and it is how we think about it, how we feel about it and ultimately, what we do with it that gives it its power, positive or otherwise. It is not desirable to be excessively rich, nor is it blessed to be extremely poor; it is just a different expression of energy and spiritual purpose. The Angels do not wish poverty or struggle on any of us, nor do they wish for us to be so focused upon amassing and holding onto money that we do not achieve anything else in our lives. The Angels simply want us to be happy, healthy, creative and in tune with our spiritual potential. They will assist with the flow of prosperity to facilitate our spiritual growth. We just need to ask.

THE KEYS TO ANGELIC PROSPERITY AND SUCCESS

Many keys to Angelic prosperity and success are specific to our individual spiritual purpose, but we can look at some general areas here and share some tools for increasing the flow of prosperity.

LOVE YOUR WORK

True prosperity comes from loving what you do and getting paid for it. There are many ways to achieve this, but the most transformational method is to love whatever work you are engaged with, regardless of whether or not it is what you ultimately wish to be doing with your life. This may seem like a tall order in some cases, but it is the most effective way of making yourself magnetic to your true goals, desires and spiritual purpose. The energy of love always has the power to transform. When you focus loving attention upon your daily activities, you make yourself available for miraculous improvements in your working life, relationships and environment. In contrast, hate, loathing, frustration and desperation can help keep you locked into negative patterns that could inhibit your career, prosperity and personal development. Frustration with your job may motivate you to want to change your company or seek a new professional role, but fuelling that frustration by placing all your attention upon it is likely to keep you attached to the problems or circumstances you most wish to be released from.

Love your present occupation and that love will
help you become magnetic to new opportunities.

A friend of mine was working as a doctor in general practice; her name was Diana. Diana did not feel appreciated or understood by her colleagues and she wanted to be in an environment where she could express a more openly spiritual dimension to her work. Her job steadily became more joyless, but she did not know how she could leave. She was nervous of making the break and losing her position and financial security. Daily, Diana focused upon what was negative about her situation and she often dreaded going into work at the beginning of her shifts. It is no surprise that she felt stuck in her situation with no obvious way of moving forward. Together, we took some time to discuss her options and decided to begin by changing the experience she was having in the present moment while focusing positively upon her future goals. We discussed ways in which she could express more of her personality and spiritual purpose within her current work environment as well as plan for new opportunities to present themselves.

One thing that Diana decided to do was brighten up her work environment. She began to take flowers into work and she made a particular effort to ensure that her consulting room was both a pleasant place for her to spend time and a safe, beautiful space for colleagues and clients to visit. Beauty and brightness were very important to her and she felt that she was contributing something of herself that, while simple, was also profoundly effective. In taking this positive action Diana felt both more loving and more in control of her situation, so her perception of her work improved dramatically. She also began to think positive, loving thoughts about her colleagues, and the combination of everything she was doing had dramatic results. The people she worked with smiled more, they became more approachable and they were also generally more supportive of her. Diana's dread of going to work dissolved and she became better able to focus upon her next career moves.

When we love we make ourselves available for the Angelic powers of transformation.

Within a short time, Diana was offered two part-time positions in environments that better suited her and where she was working with people with whom she had more in common. These opportunities allowed her to be gracefully released from her full-time job, leaving it vacant for someone else who needed it. They also gave her the security to develop private work that was both more holistic in nature and more spiritually focused. Indeed, she went on to develop more of her intuitive and psychic gifts and she now works directly with Angelic energies. As I have said before, love is Angelic, so when we fill our work with loving thoughts and feelings, we invite our Angels to touch our daily tasks and to bless our working environment. Anything that is touched and blessed by the Angels automatically transforms for the better.

WORK AND PLAY WITH THE GRACE OF THE ANGELS

Everything that is done with the grace of the Angels connects us to divine prosperity. With practice we can learn how to discern whether or not a career choice or financial opportunity is blessed by Angelic grace. If we feel moved, excited, passionate about or inspired by what we are doing, then it is most likely to be in line with our spiritual purpose and therefore, blessed by the Angels. If we feel that we are given energy, encouragement, help and guidance to take a particular position or seek a new opportunity, then we are often working with the grace of the Angels. This does not mean everything that is Angel blessed comes to us immediately and without commitment on our part, but it does mean that the process of achievement is generally fluid, the goals remain attractive and the feelings are appropriate to our inner needs and desires. When a job, career path or financial opportunity has something to offer us spiritually, our underlying motivation will remain strong even if our day-to-day enthusiasm and drive fluctuates.

The grace of the Angels comes with ease, fluidity and playfulness.

Achieving great things may take commitment or sustained effort, but if it is a struggle then something has to change. Struggle is not in line with Angelic grace. In the past, when I have struggled with a project, I have realised that I have

either chosen a path that is inappropriate for me or I have
chosen the right path but I am throwing obstacles in my own
way. Consciously, none of us would wish to throw obstacles in
our own path but being human, we may learn negative or
limiting beliefs that impede our progress, dampen our faith
and dent our confidence. The road may be straight and
clearly mapped out, but our beliefs in hard work, difficulty,
inadequacy and failure are rocks and ruts in the road that
impede our progress. Angels wish us to have lives that are
essentially playful, fluid and easy, even if there are
sometimes challenges to be faced. If we do our best to
approach our work and financial opportunities with a playful,
positive attitude, then we are more likely to be in tune with
the grace of the Angels.

The grace of the Angels can manifest as beginner's luck.
Perhaps you have had the experience of winning a game at
your first attempt or of having a door open to you the first
time you knock when others have been standing at the same
door for years, unable to cross the threshold. I would suggest
that this phenomenon, often described as beginner's luck, is a
combination of two factors. First, it is a reflection of our belief
system. When we first attempt something new we often have
not learnt that what we are aiming for is considered to be
difficult to reach, scarce or highly competitive by those with
greater experience of the territory. We succeed because we do
not believe that we will fail. It is only later when we lose our
innocence that we may convince ourselves of the difficulty of
what we are doing and that is when it all becomes a struggle.
Secondly, I believe that beginner's luck is a signal from the
Angels. When a door opens easily, when the opportunity
presented feels right and the door stays open long enough for
us to step through, it is often an indication that this step is in
line with our underlying spiritual purpose.

The Angels are always arranging prosperous
opportunities for us that are linked with our
spiritual purpose.

The Angels are always arranging prosperous opportunities for us; it is simply our job to recognise those opportunities, move beyond our fears and act accordingly. I was blessed with beginner's luck when I first began to write for commercial publishing houses. I was introduced to my literary agent Susan Mears when she was still working as a commissioning editor. Susan is a brilliantly creative, talented and intuitive woman with a lively mind and a generous heart. She and I liked each other when we first met and I told her about a book idea I had at the time. Within a few months she had become a freelance agent and she rang me up to ask if I wanted to develop my idea for publication. I created a two-page book proposal which she submitted to three publishers, all of whom wanted to publish it. By following up with a chapter of sample material, I secured a publishing contract with one of them. I have since worked with the other two companies on subsequent projects.

There are many authors I have known, more talented than I am, who struggled for years to get their first publishing contract or find a suitable agent, so why did I walk into a writing career so easily? I believe, in part, it was because I always knew I would be a writer, but I was innocent of the territory and did not hold a belief that it would be difficult to get my first book published. However, my main feeling is that being a writer, with all the learning that comes from assuming the role and the contribution that my profession has allowed me to make, is linked to a fundamental part of my spiritual purpose. As such, I owe my ease of entry into publishing to my Angelic guardians who set up my meeting with Susan, encouraged a number of commissioning editors to be receptive to my ideas and gave me the energy, inspiration and courage to follow through when presented with opportunities. I now regularly affirm for the prosperity of the Angels, listen for guidance and do my best not to throw rocks in my path. Being a human being, the latter provides me with the greatest challenge.

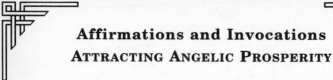

Affirmations and Invocations
ATTRACTING ANGELIC PROSPERITY

- I am blessed with the prosperity of the Angels.

- The Angels always guide me to my greatest joy.

- I am magnetic to Angelic prosperity.

- Prosperity of every kind is drawn to me.

- I am worthy of divine love and abundance.

- The Angels always help me to thrive.

- I am always fully rewarded for following my divine purpose.

- The Angels delight in showering me with an abundance of prosperous experiences.

- It is safe and easy for me   to have my needs met.

- I am always safe and secure with the grace of the Angels.

DISSOLVE YOUR FEAR OF MONEY

When my partner Justin and I talk about prosperity during some of our courses, we often discuss the fear of money that many of us have developed. Once again, the beliefs we have learnt, often early in life, may contribute to negative, fearful patterns that inhibit us. We may be scared of not having enough money and also scared of having more money than we know how to handle. We may not trust ourselves to handle money because our parents did not trust themselves with their material resources and therefore did not teach us to be comfortable working and playing with the money at our disposal. We may also be so convinced that money is a scarce commodity that we are frightened of using it in case we experience times of lack and shortage.

Whatever our particular fears, the energy of them can block the flow of prosperity as effectively as a hardened heart, fearful of being hurt, blocks the flow of love. Fear acts like a heavy shield or suit of armour to protect us from the things that we most want, need or crave. When we allow ourselves to be ruled by our fear of money, we become like a starving animal that is too traumatised to eat the food it needs to survive. With the grace of the Angels our fears can be dissolved or transformed into energy that will positively motivate us to create and enjoy what we most desire. When you receive a bill to be paid through the mail, do you dread its arrival or do you respond positively? I once knew someone who was so frightened of receiving bills that she would hide them down the back of the sofa and pretend they did not exist until she had no option but to respond to the final demand. She usually had the money to pay her bills, but her anxiety drained the pleasure from her life and inhibited her from creating new channels of prosperity and ease. When you receive your bills and when you pay them, bless them with love and ask the Angels to bless you with continuing prosperity. You will find it a much more productive approach.

When asked for help, Angels delight in dissolving our fears and helping us be available for prosperity.

Whether or not you are aware of your underlying fears, regularly ask the Angels to dissolve them and replace them with confidence and trust. You could imagine your fears to be a cumbersome suit of armour that you are wearing and picture your Angels dissolving it with golden light so that you are free to be creative, fluid and prosperous. The golden light remains with you to provide you with true protection from anything that does not serve you while making you magnetic for divine prosperity. Occasionally you may choose to write down your fears before offering them up to the Angels and positively affirming for your true needs and desires to be met. When you do this, take some time to make a note of any insights you receive and then destroy your fear list by tearing it up or safely setting light to it. It is valuable to acknowledge and express your fears but not to dwell on them. On a regular basis, you could say to the Angels,

'Thank you for dissolving my fears and helping me create new patterns of ease and prosperity.'

KEEP YOUR MONEY MOVING

When we love what we do, operate with the grace of the Angels and let go of our fears, we are better able to keep our money moving and that increases the flow of prosperity. While it may be important to invest a certain amount of your income, there is no value in doing so to the detriment of your lifestyle, dreams and spiritual goals. Money is one form of prosperity and the energy of prosperity is meant to be used to create valuable life experiences. There is no value in dreaming of becoming a musician while sitting on the money you need to buy a musical instrument and pay for music lessons. Money is intended to be used to pay for our life's adventures and to be circulated for the good of all. When we pay for something that is of value to us, we bless ourselves and the recipient of the money with the energy of prosperity. We contribute to the collective flow of prosperity and in doing so, become more available for prosperous opportunities to flow into our lives.

It does not make sense to starve the present only to feed our fears of future insecurity.

My belief in the value of circulating money does not negate the genuine need we may have to save and plan for the future. Indeed, it is wise to focus upon our long-term goals and make provision for our ongoing needs. However, I just do not see the point in tightly holding onto resources that could be used to enrich our lives and in doing so, blocking the flow of prosperous energy. It does not make sense to starve the present only to feed our fears of future insecurity. If we do have investments and savings, it is important that we review them on a regular basis, and where appropriate, move them around. In addition, we need to see the provision we make for our own training, pleasure and personal development as an investment for future prosperity and circulate our resources accordingly.

If you feel that your prosperity is stuck, do something, no matter how small, to get it moving again. There is an old piece of folklore that suggests the best way of increasing prosperity is to give something away and I have known many people who have used this wisdom to great effect. Similarly, to keep prosperous energy moving it is important to let go of anything that is old or outworn. Do not collect things that you are not going to use, instead it would be better to give them away, sell them or recycle them. If something cannot benefit someone else or be actively reused, then do not hesitate to throw it away. Similarly there is no value in holding onto ideas or ways of doing things that no longer serve you. The same principles of prosperity apply to a number of different aspects of life. If you have not worn an item of clothing for more than a year, then you are highly unlikely to wear it again and you will be better off without it. If your methods of marketing your products or services were once successful but are successful no longer, then you would be best to discard those methods and make way for a fresh approach. Letting go of anything that no longer serves you creates space for something new and better to come into your life.

- **Angels of the Elements**

Exercise

Take ten or fifteen minutes to sit somewhere comfortable and relax. Close your eyes, breathe deeply and imagine that you are in the middle of a beautiful garden. Around you is a fragrant collection of herbs, shrubs and flowers, and ahead of you is an open space that has been cleared for a sacred bonfire. The foundations of the bonfire have been laid and prepared from the dried remains of garden rubbish and it is your task to build the bonfire further by adding the dead wood of your

Exercise continued

own life to the debris that you imagine before you.

Visualise yourself placing old papers or possessions on the bonfire. These represent your outmoded ideas, your limiting beliefs and your old patterns of behaviour. See yourself building up the bonfire with old clothing that symbolises the personality traits, habits and aspects of distorted self-image that you no longer need. These are just ways you have represented yourself in the past that you have now outgrown. Your true personality is brighter and more positive than any of this could ever be. Imagine yourself adding old pieces of furniture, wooden sticks and cardboard boxes. These are metaphors for the physical objects that have provided you with a false sense of security. They are the things that you once wanted to possess and that now no longer hold any value for you.

Once the bonfire has been built high and firm upon the earth, take a last look at the dead wood that you have been carrying with you in your life. Some of the ideas, beliefs, habits, desires, possessions and patterns of behaviour may well have served you in the past, but if they no longer serve you now, their energy is only going to hold you back. Bless them all with love and, in your mind, ask the Angels to help you clear them from your life and help you to become available for new and better experiences.

Invoke the Angels of fire and imagine them gathering to set light to your bonfire. Visualise yourself watching as the red-orange flame transforms all that is old and outworn in your life, converting the energy of that dead wood into something new and positive. From a safe distance continue to add more stale ideas and outmoded beliefs and watch them combust.

'Angels of fire transform my life for the better. Enlighten and inspire me now and forever more.'

Exercise continued

Invoke the Angels of the air and imagine them gathering to transport the smoke and ether from the fire to where it can best create some good in the world. See yourself watching the smoke rise and picture the gentle breezes taking the transformed energy of your old thoughts and beliefs away for ever. At the same time ask the Angels of the air to deliver the message to the heavens that you are now available for new prosperity, adventure and joy.

'Angels of air release me from the past, refresh my ideas and transport me to my glorious future.'

Watch the bonfire burn down to ash and then invoke the Angels of water. Imagine the water Angels coming to you with a sensual downpour of summer rain and picture the ash from the fire being washed to where it is most needed in the garden. The sweet water douses the dying embers of the fire and cleanses your mind, body and emotions of any residual influences from the past that no longer serve your highest good.

'Angels of water cleanse and nourish me. Wash away the past and help me to drink from the chalice of new wisdom, inspiration and creativity.'

Invoke the Angels of the earth and imagine them receiving the fertile ash that the water Angels bring to them. The ash from your bonfire, transported by the soft summer rains, nourishes the earth and stimulates new life, new growth and an abundance of new things. Soon your garden will be filled with more fragrant herbs, flowers and shrubs and your life will be blessed with prosperity.

'Angels of earth stabilise and support me. Provide me with the fertile ground to seed new prosperity and help me to reap the abundant rewards that await me.'

Exercise continued

When this process feels complete, thank the Angels of the elements for their loving support and take a few moments to plan your next move. If there is something that you need to release physically from your life, such as a clutter of old business correspondence or some old clothing, then schedule some time to attend to it. If you have some new ideas that could stimulate your prosperity, then make a note of them and schedule a time to follow them through.   **Exercise** •

End

======= INVOCATION =======

Angels of Prosperity

Angels of prosperity bless me so that my spiritual growth and my material success are truly aligned.

May my work reflect my spiritual purpose and my spiritual purpose guide me to work that is truly prosperous and fulfilling.

May I easily manifest the money I need to live in joy and abundance.

May I be guided to all opportunities that will benefit me and benefit the people I love and care for.

May I be guided to all opportunties that help me to benefit the wider community of humans and Angels in which I live.

Give me the strength, courage and inspiration to transform all of my opportunities into great successes.

May money, love and peace of mind flow into my life with equal abundance.

May I always live with the joy of true prosperity in all its many forms.

I give thanks for my prosperity and thanks in abundance for the blessings of the Angels.

Chapter Five
Angels of Love, Loss and Laughter

It is you I am seeking, the man of a thousand faces,
And every one the face of an Angel.

It is you that I came to meet, the woman who
walks steadily,
Away from the shadows and into the light,
And every step the footfall of an Angel.

As I look at your face, I look in the mirror,
As I walk with you I also walk,
Steadily into the light.

Being with you, I see you for who you really are,
And it is easy to fall in love.

Being with you, I know that I am Angel borne,
And I am also blessed with the face of an Angel.

David Lawson, 1998

ANGELIC RELATIONSHIPS

Just as we each have the potential to awaken and develop the
Angelic aspects of our consciousness, life purpose and
personality, we all have the potential to awaken those
qualities within our relationships. Because all connections
between people are inherently spiritual, every human contact

contains the seeds of an Angelic relationship. Perhaps the relationships that are most overtly Angelic are simply those where a similarity of Angelic purpose brings people together. Indeed, my definition of 'a company of Angels' is a collection of two or more individuals drawn together to fulfil a greater Angelic purpose.

So how do we make ourselves available for Angelic relationships and how may we enhance the Angelic potential available to us within all of our existing human connections? Here is my five point action plan for creating love, romance and friendship that is truly blessed by the divine.

1. Become Magnetic to Angelic Relationships

All relationships are essentially Angel blessed, we just need to become magnetic to the Angelic qualities that are there within them and then nurture that Angelic potential until it grows. This principle is essentially the same for existing relationships, new relationships and the relationships to which you currently aspire. When you focus upon the Angelic qualities within yourself, and do your best to keep your eyes and ears open for the many miracles that occur around you in your daily life, you automatically make yourself more available for the Angelic potential within your relationships. Angels attract Angels and Angelic people have a magnetism for others who are on a complementary spiritual path.

Angels of a feather flock together.

Whenever I lead courses, I am frequently amazed at the similarity of purpose that exists between the individuals who attend. At my healing, personal development and self-healing groups I often have a number of people turn up who are dealing with similar medical conditions, relationship issues or family belief patterns. It is as if the Angels have guided these people together to support, inspire and learn from each other so that they can best make positive changes in their lives. In my psychic and spiritual development courses I often attract individuals whom the Angels have drawn together because they have similar gifts or abilities. Learning together helps them to strengthen those abilities and inspires them with the confidence to express their innate spiritual potential.

I have a secret that I have not previously shared with anyone. Ever ready to enlist the help of the Angels and to make the most of the similarity of purpose that is present within each collection of individuals, I begin to address the higher spiritual potential of the group before my courses begin. The night before each of my workshops, I ask the Angels to guide my course participants to the venue in question, keeping each person safe enroute, and I ask that they may each arrive with an open heart so that they may learn something valuable from everyone present. During the process of the course, many of my participants experience a remarkable degree of spiritual recognition of each other, even if they have not previously met.

Just as the individual participants who make up a group on any one of my courses often 'mirror' each other's needs, beliefs and special qualities, their problems and concerns often reflect issues and spiritual lessons relevant to myself and my associates. When my partner Justin Carson was diagnosed with a form of cancer growing behind his palate, the number of people drawn to us who were also dealing with issues related to past or present cancerous conditions increased dramatically. In addition to the swapping of notes on medical treatments and complementary therapies, the shared experience helped everyone to come to terms with the emotional and spiritual aspects of his or her illness, Justin included.

Our needs, wounds, skills, talents and special qualities make us magnetic to other people who reflect our deepest issues and unique spiritual potential.

Recently, when I resolved to heal myself of a mild eating disorder, which had become more apparent during the stress of caring for a number of people close to me with potentially serious illnesses, I found that I had become magnetic to others who were successfully learning to manage food addictions. In some cases, the eating disorders that other people were seeking to heal were superficially different from my own, but the underlying causes were often remarkably similar. Indeed, many of us were highly intuitive people, some of us were positively Angelic and most were born carers who were looking to fill the void of our own frustrated needs and desires. In a similar way, when I am developing a new skill, ability or area of interest, I can guarantee that someone will appear in one of my groups with similar talents, interests or aspirations.

Every group I have worked with has been unique. Groups as well as individuals have their own special qualities and personalities. Each collection of individuals comes together to fulfil a divine purpose, whether or not this is immediately apparent. This is true of life in general. Professional groups, departmental teams, student groups, social circles and especially families are all formed to fulfil a spiritual purpose that often runs deeper than the obvious connection. For example, a sales team may be formed to market and distribute a particular product and superficially this may appear to be the purpose of the group. At a deeper level, however, this group of individuals may have been drawn together to learn patience, tolerance, co-operation and compassion from each other or they may be working together to refine and strengthen their powers of communication.

A common intention can give a group an enhanced spiritual purpose and a pronounced Angelic connection.

The difference between any group of people drawn together for a common purpose and a group that comes together to participate in a personal development programme or work of love is often one of awareness and intention. When two or more people meet with a conscious intention to heal themselves, improve their lives, develop their intuitive or psychic abilities or grow spiritually, then the connection formed is likely to have an enhanced spiritual purpose. When the group intention is also focused upon sending the energy of love, peace and healing into the world to improve the lives of others, then the connection is undoubtedly Angelic in nature.

Whether you are seeking to be part of a group with an Angelic purpose or whether you wish to create a number of friendships that reflect your growing Angelic nature, it helps to boost your personal Angelic magnetism in a number of ways. It is certainly a good idea to ask the Angels for their support by beginning to use some powerful positive thought techniques that will also train you to be available for the transformation that is bound to occur within all of your relationships. Whether you wish to create a new romantic relationship that is blessed by the Angels or to awaken the Angelic potential that is lying dormant within your existing romantic relationship or marriage, increasing your own Angelic magnetism is an excellent place to start. Use the exercise and affirmations that follow on a daily basis. Regular practice for the next two weeks will help create your initial momentum. Return to them periodically whenever your relationships need a boost.

- ## Your Angel Notice-board

Exercise

Take ten or fifteen minutes to sit somewhere comfortable and relax. Close your eyes, breathe deeply and imagine that you have an Angel notice-board. This is a billboard where you can advertise your wants, needs and desires for all passing Angels to see. Visualise or create this in your mind as best you can. It is not important to have a strong mental image of this, just an impression of a notice-board or the concept of one is enough for the exercise to work beautifully for you. However, it may help you to decide what colour this notice-board is, what it is made of and how it might be decorated. Imagine it big so that there is plenty of space for all your requests and so that you can advertise them in

Exercise continued

large letters. Make it a notice-board that will be easy for Angels to see and take notice of. What is more, imagine that this board has an Angelic fragrance such as a delicious smell of jasmine or rose and mentally surround it with the sounds of beautiful music

Visualise yourself writing the words:

- I am a magnet for Angelic relationships

and pasting them on to your notice-board.

If you wish to enhance the Angelic qualities within your existing relationships, then imagine yourself writing some appropriate notices to add to your board. For example, you may wish for a greater sense of spiritual connection between yourself and your life partner, so you could imagine yourself pasting up a notice that says,

- I wish to create a greater sense of intimacy and spiritual connection in my relationship with my husband/wife/boyfriend/girlfriend/partner ...

Alternatively, you may wish for a greater spiritual understanding between yourself and other members of your family such as your parents, your children or your siblings, so you could imagine writing a notice to address this. You may say,

- With the blessings of the Angels, I now create a greater spiritual understanding between myself and my mother/daughter/son/brother, etc.

Obviously, you just need to use the words appropriate to the relationship and to the specific

Exercise continued

needs or desires that you have. As you do this, listen carefully for any messages you receive in the form of images, thoughts, words, feelings or impulses. During the days that follow, you may have a sense that you need to do something practical to help facilitate your goals. When we wish for changes in our relationships, we may be moved to begin by making appropriate changes within ourselves.

If you wish to attract new people to you who have a similar Angelic purpose, then use the notice-board accordingly. You may wish for a support group of friends with a similar spiritual focus to your own or you may wish the Angels to help you find that one special person with whom you would like to share your life. You may imagine yourself writing,

- I am always surrounded by supportive people with similar interests and a similar spiritual vision to my own.

Or you may say,

- I now attract an available and appropriate man/woman for a relationship that is loving, pleasurable, romantic and blessed by the Angels.

Whether you wish to enhance an existing relationship or attract a new one, remember that the Angels cannot and will not make anyone do anything that he or she does not wish to. However, your Angelic messengers will pass on your requests to the higher consciousness of everyone concerned and they will help facilitate the changes of thought, mood, action and communication required for success. Some requests may be granted immediately while others may take a little time. The timing is

Exercise continued

usually set by your underlying spiritual purpose and your willingness to follow your highest spiritual guidance.

Regularly revisit your notice-board to adjust your written requests so that they may reflect your changing needs and remember to thank the Angels for any miraculous changes within your relationships, no matter how unconnected some of those changes may initially appear to be. To enhance the process you may wish to use some appropriate affirmations.

Exercise • End

Affirmations and Invocations

ATTRACTING ANGELIC RELATIONSHIPS

- Angels of love now open my heart to the divine.

- My relationships are always divinely protected and inspired.

- I easily see the Angelic qualities within other people.

- I am magnetic to Angelic people.

- All of my relationships are Angelic.

- My relationships are inspired by divine purpose.

- I love the Angel in you and celebrate the Angel in myself.

- Angels of a feather flock together.

- I am always surrounded by Angelic friends.

- I am always drawn to groups with a powerful Angelic purpose.

2. Open Your Heart

Many of us go through life with a closed heart and then wonder why we have problems creating and maintaining loving relationships. To be available for loving relationships that are also profoundly Angelic, it is important to learn to open our hearts in a way that is appropriate for our higher goals and spiritual potential. A truly open heart is not the bleeding heard of a martyr or the open wound of someone who has been hurt and whose belief system is charged with the expectation of being hurt again, instead, it is the heart of someone whose level of self-love and divine trust allows a free sharing of the love and joy that is readily available to us all.

It is not surprising that we close our hearts. I have not met a single human being who has not experienced at least a degree of pain in his or her life. Whether we have lost someone we love or have become disillusioned when our love and friendship have been unrequited or, in some cases, actively abused, we all have many reasons to close our hearts. While everyone's story is different, the underlying reason for a closed heart is often remarkably similar from one person to another. We all fear pain and wish to defend ourselves from experiences that may prove to be hurtful or that may leave us emotionally vulnerable to loss.

We close our hearts from self-defence, but the only real defence is a combination of self-trust and the protection of the Angels.

In my own life I have experienced the pain and grief that comes with nursing people I love as they face the challenge of potentially life-threatening illnesses. I have also experienced the death of close friends and know first hand that it is very tempting to want to build a wall in front of my heart so that I never allow myself to become as emotionally involved again. To love is to open yourself up to loss or distress when something happens to the object of your loving attention, and a small degree of self-defence is probably healthy. It is a natural expression of our basic survival impulse. However, we often have a tendency to greatly exceed this basic impulse and in doing so, we often cause or accentuate the pain that we most wish to avoid. When we attempt to defend ourselves from pain, we often make ourselves more magnetic to painful experiences and less available for the love we most desire. The only real defence comes from opening our hearts, learning to trust our ability to handle whatever life brings and enlisting the protection of the Angels.

Keeping our hearts closed starves us of the expression of love that we all need for our emotional health. The energy we invest in defending ourselves blocks the channels of our creativity while keeping us more focused upon pain than joy. Simply put, what we resist persists. This does not mean that the best protection is no protection; rather it means that we need to deal with our feelings, be very loving to ourselves and continue to express the love and joy that is an integral part of our Angelic nature. When we open our hearts we also open ourselves up to the love of the Angels and we allow our guides and guardians to bless us with emotional healing. An open heart heals faster. It radiates the light that will attract new love, new hope and a greater spiritual contact between ourselves and everyone we meet.

The spiritual lessons that come from our impulse to give and receive love are often the most powerful and transformational of them all.

Our guardian Angels are continually presenting us with opportunities to open our hearts. The spiritual lessons that come from our impulse to give and receive love are often the most powerful and transformational of them all. It is important that we explore and learn from the full range of feelings that our capacity to love awakens within us. With the help of the Angels, you may open your heart safely and fulfil your greatest spiritual potential. You were created to be loved. The Angels love you and wish you to have the joy that love can bring. It is simply your job to step out of your own way so that you can receive all the wonderful feelings that are available to you.

• Open Your Heart Visualisation

Exercise

Take ten or fifteen minutes to sit somewhere comfortable and relax. Close your eyes, breathe deeply and imagine an Angel of love hovering above you. This Angel may be one of your guardians or may simply have come to you to help you transform your relationships at this time. Notice how it feels to receive the love and support of this Angel. Are there any sounds, words, images or fragrances that are associated with this divine being? Use your imagination to build the feeling, concept or picture of this Angelic presence.

Imagine your Angel of love touching your heart with a hand, wing or beam of golden light. Breathe deeply and allow yourself to receive the love, healing and reassurance that is offered you. Visualise the whole of your chest expanding and relaxing to receive more Angel light and allow your body to fill with a deep sense of peace. Your Angel dissolves all pain from your heart and heals all old wounds left over from past relationships. Your heart is strengthened and brightened to allow you to become magnetic for more love within all of your relationships. You find it easier to give love, easier to express your loving feelings and easier to forgive and let go of the past.

Visualise your heart and your chest continuing to expand and filling with light of many colours: turquoise, blue, orange, purple, daffodil yellow, vibrant red and bright sea green. Picture your whole body relaxing and expanding. As you breathe in, imagine your body drinking in more love from your Angel, transmitted as swirling, shimmering lights of gold, silver and rose pink. A gold and silver web of light forms loosely around your heart to protect you so that you may safely be open hearted wherever you go.

Exercise continued

Knowing that you cannot make anyone do anything that is against his or her will, ask your Angel of love to safely open the hearts of the people close to you so that your relationships can grow in love and understanding. One by one, picture each of your friends touched by this Angel. Imagine the hearts of partners, lovers and family members opening to Angel light. You may even see colleagues, employers, clients or others with whom you have a professional relationship touched and healed by the love of the Angels.

If there is someone with whom you are having problems, the Angel of love can help to heal the situation and open up new areas of communication between you. Ask this Angel, and all of your guardians, to dispel all of the negative thoughts and bad feeling that you have generated with this person. You could picture this as clearing away a cloud of dense grey fog with an abundance of golden light and sunshine. Once the fog has cleared, see and feel your Angel touching both your heart and the heart of the other person so that you may become more loving towards each other. Ask all of your Angels to give you the guidance you need to bring about a safe and happy resolution to your problems and to heal the disharmony you have experienced. It could be that you need do nothing more than let go and trust, or you may feel moved to open up a new dialogue with this person. Proceed gently, with love and respect for all concerned, yourself included.

When this process feels complete, thank your Angel of love, and all your guardians, for their help. Make a note of any guidance you received and act upon it in the best way possible. **Exercise • End**

3. Discover Your Mutual Purpose

When we marry or live with someone, we may be drawn to be with that person because of a similarity of underlying spiritual purpose. To enhance our relationship and enable it to grow, we may benefit from exploring that mutual purpose and nurturing it. Many couples have a common purpose of bringing children into the world and caring for them until they are old enough to make their own way. If those couples have begun to explore the other facets of their mutual purpose early in this process, then, when the children grow up and spread their wings, there is a greater chance of the relationship surviving and continuing to grow in new directions. Similarly, friendships are built on a purpose that may be both mutual and parallel. Good, potent friendships are often based upon two or more people moving in a similar spiritual direction for a period of their lives. This is a little like two trains travelling on tracks that cross the same terrain and are laid down side by side for part of their route. Once the tracks split and diverge the relationship has fulfilled its purpose and the individuals move in their different directions.

The greater the connection between our goals and
their spiritual core, the more Angelic our
relationships can become.

Angelic relationships, whether a marriage, a friendship or any other connection between people, thrive on finding a common vision. For some couples, having children is the cornerstone of their common vision. For other partnerships, whether heterosexual or same sex, having children may not be key to their common vision or may not be a desired option and other goals emerge to express the mutual purpose of the relationship. The common vision of a couple may include the creation of a business, building a home together, the furtherance of each person's individual career, study, travel or simply, and most profoundly, mutual love and companionship. All of these goals and visions, while important in themselves, are the tangible expressions of a deeper spiritual purpose.

The greater the connection between our goals and their spiritual core, the more Angelic our relationships can become. We can strengthen that connection through developing our conscious awareness of mutual purpose, effective communication with our partners and friends and the expression of shared values within all our relationships.

Regularly ask the Angels to strengthen and enhance the purpose of each key relationship you have in your life and affirm that you will attract new people whose spiritual goals complement your own. When asked, the Angels delight in setting up meetings between individuals whose individual purposes can be mutually developed. Similarly, the Angels can be enlisted to restimulate the mutual purpose of two or more people whose relationship is floundering. When relationships are effectively renegotiated to take account of each individual's changing needs, goals and spiritual purpose, a new sense of common purpose can often be established. Successful, long-term relationships often thrive because equal importance is given to joint and individual goals. They also thrive because all parties involved are willing to forgive the past and find new ways of relating to each other.

Angelic relationships thrive on forgiveness,
imagination and a willingness to make a fresh start.

I once lost patience with a friend I loved very much but whom I judged to be erratic, unreliable and excessively needy. After an incident where I felt she had let me down badly, I decided that I did not want the friendship to continue, so I did little to encourage her when she telephoned me and I did not instigate any further contact between us. I hoped that the relationship would gently fade away and die. After a few weeks had passed without much contact, I went away for a weekend of quiet meditation. During the second day of my retreat, I took part in a long meditation that included mentally blessing a number of people in my life with peace of mind and joy. I included a number of friends and family members in my blessings and was enjoying the sense of peace that was growing in my own mind as I did this. It was not until I was nearing completion of this process that my peaceful state was temporarily disrupted by a clear inner vision of my estranged friend.

I attempted to push the image of this woman to one side and carry on sending thoughts of peace to others, but she kept coming back to my mind. It did not matter what I thought of, she would not go away and I became more and more irritated by her. After a while, I surrendered and began to bless her with peace of mind and joy, just like the others. At first, nothing happened and then, as I continued to send her peace, my friend's image grew brighter and clearer until it changed into a vision of a golden Angel, shimmering with the light of love. I became infused with feelings of loving acceptance and my own peace of mind returned, embellished by this experience.

The Angels may help to bring out the best qualities of our relationships.

I did not immediately contact my friend on my return home, but within a couple of weeks, she telephoned me and I noticed that I felt totally different towards her. We soon put the past behind us and began to create a relationship that has become more meaningful and more supportive with each passing year. It was this friend who subsequently held my hand through the most challenging period of my life and who has proved be fully committed to me during my times of need. The connection between us is like the relationship between two members of the same spiritual family and we can often say things to each other that we cannot talk about to anyone else. Friendships like this are golden and Angel blessed.

4. Laugh Together and Bless Each Other

Angels love laughter, and humour is very important in creating Angelic relationships, but it does need to be the right kind of humour. For a man with a good memory, I do not seem to be able to remember jokes and funny stories, but I like to think that I have a well-developed sense of humour. Perhaps one of the reasons I forget jokes is that so many of them are at the expense of other people and while my humour can be as wicked as the next person and I am certainly far from perfect, I do feel that laughter is supposed to heal and lift the spirit rather than wound it.

Many relationships seem to rely on humour that is wounding to the other person. I have watched married couples enact a pattern of behaviour that consists of one person being the comedian and the other the stooge, or the butt of jokes. This is a relationship pattern that is jointly created, with both parties equally responsible for the roles they assume. In the short term it may create laughter, in the long term it rarely lifts the spirit or strengthens the love between two people.

Angelic laughter is a response to the pure fun and joy of being alive.

The Angelic humour that contributes to Angelic relationships is quite different from the jokes made at another's expense. Angelic laughter is a response to the pure joy and fun of being alive. It often comes in a moment of recognition between two or more people. It is the laughter that surfaces when we catch someone's eye and know that we are both responding to the absurdity of the experience we are sharing. It is the fun that comes from doing something new and responding to the thrill of a new sensation. Angelic humour is connected to the delight that we feel when we are switched on and passionate about life. When we laugh with the Angels, we strengthen our spirits and lift our hearts to touch the divine.

Babies and small children are great teachers of Angelic humour. I once watched a little boy of about three years of age demonstrate the joy of Angelic humour. He was dressed in a raincoat and bright red wellington boots and he was accompanying his mother on a walk through some park land. It had recently rained and there were big puddles of water everywhere. As you may already know, somewhere there is an unwritten law that when we are three it is our duty to jump in every single puddle we see and this young man was observing this law to the letter. Jumping in puddles was obviously a recent discovery for this little boy because with every splash his little face filled up with the thrill of new sensation and adventure. He laughed with unbridled joy and I swear I heard some Angels laugh too.

The joy and laughter of small children can provide us with a powerful demonstration of Angelic humour.

A few years ago, someone gave me two photographs of a baby seeing his reflection in a mirror for the first time. In the first picture, this baby boy, who was just old enough to sit upright, is placed in front on a large mirror and he notices the image of his reflection. In the second picture he experiences the realisation that this is his own image that he is looking at and his joy of recognition is wonderful to behold. This boy is beaming with delight and his eyes are filled with laughter. We may all experience this joy of recognition, both of ourselves and others, when we allow ourselves to be light-hearted and touched by the pure wonder of being alive. Within our relationships, it is important to regularly bless each other with loving, joyful thoughts and find things to do together that allow us to be genuinely playful. The ways of generating spirals of Angelic laughter will be as unique as the tastes, needs and desires of the individuals concerned and are well worth exploring. Ask the Angels for their help and inspiration.

5. Be Willing to Let Go

If we make ourselves available for their love, Angels will comfort us through times of loss and heartache. To continue to love we need to be willing to let go and to deal with the natural feelings of loss and grief that we all experience at some time in our lives. All relationships come to an end. It is a natural part of our spiritual growth and evolution. Without endings there cannot be new beginnings and life would become stagnant. We would cease to learn anything new and block opportunities to become more aligned to our Angelic potential. It is important to let go, acknowledge our feelings and trust the miracle of life to bring us what we truly need.

When particular members of a group have learnt all that they can from the team of people they have been drawn to, they often move on or at the very least, redefine their purpose so that they can learn or contribute something a little different. Some groups stay together for life, with the members periodically defining and redefining their roles while other groups fulfil their purpose in a short time and the individuals move on to new challenges. This dynamic is the same for marriages, love affairs, business partnerships and friendships. It is also similar to the process that occurs when children grow up, express more of their independence and when they are ready, spread their wings and fly from the nest. It is often our ability to deal with these changes and adapt to our present opportunities that makes the difference between a personal mastery of life and a life of resistance, denial and frustration.

Death is both a spiritual beginning and a physical loss. As we let go, the love of the Angels continues to grow and thrive.

Being Angel guided and inspired, I usually feel spiritually peaceful about the death of someone I love. I do genuinely believe that death is just the beginning of a greater spiritual adventure and, as such, I often find it easy to be reasonable and philosophical about what is happening to the people I care about. However, no degree of spiritual understanding can cancel out the very human feelings we all have when we lose those we love or when we bear witness to their suffering. We physically miss people when they are no longer with us and because we love them so much, we often have a very human desire to take away the pain that others experience.

From my observation, the healthiest people are those who give expression to both their reasonable and their unreasonable voices during times of loss or separation. To continue to love with all our hearts, we need to recognise that, in addition to our Angelic awareness and spiritual beliefs, we have our human needs and grief. Some of our thoughts and feelings may be contradictory, but we need to give space for them all. The Angels will take care of the rest. Love that is truly Angelic continues to grow and thrive beyond any illusion of physical separation.

• Let Go to the Angels

Exercise

This exercise is equally appropriate at the end of a friendship, the end of a business partnership or when we have experienced a divorce or separation. It may also be adapted to begin to address the loss we feel when someone we love dies.

Find a quiet, comfortable place to sit and relax. Make sure that you are not going to be disturbed for a while and take a few long, slow, deep breaths to settle yourself before you begin. Read through this exercise a couple of times to familiarise yourself with the key points before proceeding. As always, do not worry about getting every detail correct and in the sequence as written, just read through the details, breathe deeply, allow your eyes to close and let your mind wander, the Angels will do the rest.

Imagine yourself standing in a beautiful room filled with Angels and, in your mind's eye, look around you to familiarise yourself with your location. This hall of Angels is filled with bright light, beautiful colours, luxurious fragrances and melodic sounds. There is a feeling of peace, harmony and comfort that touches the core of your spirit.

Some of the Angels are your own Angelic guardians, some are the guardians of the person you are separating from and some are just here to offer help

Exercise continued

to you both during this transition. Acknowledge them all for their loving support.

Visualise the person in question materialising in front of you and imagine them as they were when you last saw them. Picture this person's hair, clothing and posture and take a few moments to look them in the eyes. Spend some time talking to this person and saying anything that has been left unsaid between you. You may do this aloud or with your thoughts, but either way, do your best to express what you are feeling, whether love, anger, sadness, relief, grief or a number of other emotions. Allow yourself plenty of space to do this before giving this person permission to move on to the next part of their journey or adventure. Ask the Angels to guide them and help them on their way and ask that you may be safely reunited again in the future if it be appropriate for you both.

Picture this person filled and surrounded with bright Angelic light and accompanied by a number of Angels as their image dissolves from the room. Imagine them liberated and able to fulfil their highest spiritual purpose and potential. Take a few deep breaths and bring your attention back to yourself. A number of Angels are around you to bring you comfort and to guide you towards some new experiences of love and spiritual fulfilment. Ask them for anything you need and thank them before bringing your attention back to the present moment and opening your eyes. Take some time with your thoughts and feelings before doing anything else.

If you need help coming to terms with grief, bereavement and loss, then you may wish to seek bereavement counselling. Your doctor, healer or complementary practitioner may be able to guide you towards the relevant organisations in your area.

Exercise • End

INVOCATION

Attracting Angel Love

May the Angels bless me with an abundance of loving relationships.

May all my relationships be blessed with divine love and harmony.

I ask that I be drawn to other people whose spiritual purpose complements my own.

I ask that I may help to awaken the Angelic qualities within others and strengthen those qualities within myself.

I am always surrounded by Angels in human form.

My guardian Angels always guide me to loving, supportive people.

I thank my Angels for the gift of laughter within all of my relationships.

I ask that I may become magnetic to Angelic love in every moment of the day and night.

I ask that I may bless the lives of others with the love and laughter of the Angels.

Chapter Six
Angels of Healing and Compassion

I am the woman who lighteneth the darkness, I
have come to lighten the darkness, it is lightened
doubly.

I have lightened the darkness, I have overthrown
the destroyers, I have adored those who are in the
darkness.

I have made to stand those who weep, who hid
their faces, who had sunk down.
They looked upon me then ... I am a woman.

From *The Egyptian Book of the Dead*

HEALING WITH FIRE AND LIGHT

There are many stories about Angels visiting the darkest or
most dangerous places to bring comfort to the human souls
who have found themselves there, whether through choice,
misadventure or birth. Prisons, war zones, areas of famine
and dark nights of the soul are said to attract the ministry of
Angels who offer the healing and protection of spiritual fire.
Perhaps the most popular story of this kind is the biblical tale
of Daniel in the lions' den. Daniel was cast into a den of lions
for reasons of political jealousy. His only true offence was to
break the new law of King Darius by praying to God every
day. Indeed, the King himself was tricked by politicians who

were envious of Daniel's position and popularity into creating a law that would condemn him. Daniel was cast into the lions' den for a night and the entrance was sealed with a stone. During the night, God sent one of his Angels to close the lions' mouths. When the King returned to the den in the morning, he found Daniel unharmed and commanded that he be released and allowed to prosper.

Missions of healing and protection are fundamental to the work of the Angels. Those of us who choose to offer care, healing and support to other people are often the human envoys of an Angelic mission. Whether you are a doctor, a nurse, a spiritual healer, a complementary therapist or, more simply, someone who offers help to an elderly neighbour or listens to a friend in distress, you may find that you are on an errand of Angelic mercy. Those who provide healing or protection for others are accompanied by Angels as they go about their tasks. This does not mean that there is no need to take care of ourselves as we take care of other people; nothing could be further from the truth. The world has suffered too many martyrs who deny their own needs. However, it does mean that we are aided in all that we do. Indeed, there are times when our presence alone allows the Angels to fulfil their divine purpose and create healing solutions, even when there is no physical help we can offer.

Healing is an essential part of human spiritual evolution.

Healing is much more than repairing a broken wrist, bandaging a wound, regenerating tissue or curing an infection. Healing is an essential part of human spiritual evolution. We are all on a healing journey. Some of us may be focused upon casting out our inner demons, others may be seeking to fill a void that we feel within and many are simply looking for ways to be happier. As humanity continues to develop, the nature of healing is changing. What was once an impulse to fix what is broken is now an impetus to grow towards the light. Healing is symptomatic of our quest to become more gloriously expressive, expansive and Angelic. It is much bigger and more positive than many of its daily applications would suggest. Rather than just acting as a sticking plaster for the ills of the world, healing is connected to the transformation of the spirit as it becomes whole and grows to embody its greater divine potential.

THE GIFT OF ANGELIC PROTECTION

Angels provide protection for us in many different situations and environments. Sometimes they protect by cheering the human spirit and boosting the natural impulse to survive so that individuals in danger are given the will required to ensure their survival. At other times, Angels protect by influencing matter. For example, they may physically move an object, person or vehicle to minimise the damage to life and limb brought about by the impact of a car crash. Angels may also influence the timing of an event to allow someone to escape from danger or they may stand between an individual and a potential attacker. In my own life, I have benefited from Angelic protection on a number of occasions.

The Angels may heighten our senses and guide our actions during times of threat or danger.

I was once threatened at knife point when I was walking home. I was living temporarily in west London and was returning to my lodgings from a rehearsal for a performance piece I was creating with some friends. At that time in my life I was working as an actor and performance poet. I was carrying a bag filled with original poetry that formed the basis of the script for the forthcoming show. As I walked I was preoccupied with my thoughts and I did not pay full attention to my surroundings, but my instincts swiftly told me that I was being watched. I sensed that it would not be appropriate to run away or make any sudden move and a voice inside my head told me to keep walking, stay peaceful and I would be safe. I was soon surrounded by a number of young men and one was brandishing a knife.

Although I could feel the adrenaline rushing through my body, I felt as if someone were shielding me from harm. Rather than panicking, I became quite calm and my senses heightened. Without stopping to look, I knew the position of everyone around me and I felt quite in control. The man threatening me with a knife told me to hand over everything I was carrying. I told him that I had a small amount of money in my wallet and that he was welcome to it but that he could not have my bag. I was only carrying £15 which, at the time, I couldn't really afford to lose, but I knew that money was easier to replace than my creative work. Without breaking my stride, I handed him my wallet and then took it back from him once he had removed the money. Disappointed with his prize, he asked me what else I was carrying and I repeated that my bag contained nothing of value to him and that he could not have it. I then told him and his friends to leave me alone and I continued to walk homewards.

The Angels may shield us with love until it is safe
to let go.

I did not look back but I sensed the group of young men disengage from me and I felt strangely elated. I was amazed by my calm, assertive approach to this threat and I felt as if a shield of love was surrounding me all the way home. It was only when I was safely behind the locked front door of my lodgings that my anxieties surfaced and I was able to contemplate the vulnerability of my situation. I also thanked the Angels for my good fortune. I had walked through this experience without receiving a scratch or bruise on my body and without losing anything that held any real value for me. All I lost was £15, although my confidence was dented temporarily. My Angels soon gave me the opportunity to move to a safer part of town, but the memory of their protection on this and other occasions has stayed with me.

We may all invite Angelic protection whenever we feel vulnerable, unsure of ourselves or in need of support. As always, we are simply required to ask for help and be willing to act upon the guidance we receive. We may even ask the

Angels to guard our home or protect our belongings and we can be quite light-hearted about it. I regularly ask for some little sprites to look after my car wherever it is parked, some Angels to protect me and my loved ones when we are travelling and some guides to direct us safely home again. The Angels often provide me with a good sense of direction even when I am reading the road map upside down. I do my best to remember to thank all my Angels afterwards; everyone likes to be thanked!

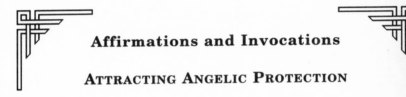

Affirmations and Invocations

ATTRACTING ANGELIC PROTECTION

- I am always safe, loved and protected.

- The Angels protect me wherever I go.

- I am shielded by the light of the Angels.

- I am magnetic to the peace and grace that exists within all situations.

- I trust my instincts to keep me safe.

- I trust the Angels to guide me safely throughout the day.

- My Angels watch over me as I sleep.

- I seek and accept the sanctuary of the Angels.

- I am in a golden cocoon of protective Angelic love.

- My Angels bring peace, diplomacy and healing to all aspects of my life.

• Invoking Angelic Protection

Any of the images contained within this exercise can be repeated at times when you are feeling in need of Angelic protection. For instance, you may quickly ask to be surrounded by Angelic protectors when you find yourself in an environment that does not appear safe, such as a poorly lit street or darkened parking area. However, it is best to begin using this exercise in its entirety within the comfort of your own home and ahead of any specific need you may have for protection. To be most effective it is important that you focus upon thoughts of safety and peace rather than on your fears of attack, accident, robbery, assault or injury. If you establish a firm belief that you are always safe and fully protected by your divine guardians, then the Angels will help you create ongoing safety as part of the reality of your life.

Find a quiet, comfortable place to sit and relax. Make sure that you are not going to be disturbed and take a few long, slow, deep breaths to settle yourself before you begin. Read through this exercise a couple of times to familiarise yourself with the key points before proceeding. Allow your eyes to softly close and use your imagination to paint the picture, build the feeling or frame the concept of the following sequence:

Visualise yourself in a cocoon of golden light energy. You may imagine this as a bubble of light, or a cocoon-like web of golden threads, or a shield of pure gold that protects you on all sides, including the areas above your head and below your feet. Take a few moments to build the image, feeling or concept of this golden structure before proceeding. Within your cocoon of gold you are filled with a sense of peace, strength and stability. Imagine that your feet are placed firmly upon the earth, even if you are about to travel in a moving vehicle such as a car, boat or aeroplane.

Next, visualise yourself surrounded by four Angels of protection. If you are feeling particularly vulnerable and in need of high-level protection you could imagine this to be the four Archangels. Visualise Gabriel walking in front of you and ask him to be your eyes and ears and to clear your pathway. Sense Raphael behind you, guarding your back, bringing you support and illuminating your blind spots. Ask Michael to guard your right side, using his sword of truth to dispel your fears and bring clarity to your situation. Picture Uriel protecting your left side with a torch of spiritual fire to banish the darkness.

Your own guardian Angels bring you a wand of light to create some further protection. Imagine yourself pointing your wand in front of you and then turning your body around anticlockwise, three hundred and sixty degrees, so that you can draw a circle with it that will connect the four points occupied by the four Angels. As you do this, a circle of spiritual fire springs up around you to help keep you safe. See yourself completely protected with a cocoon of light, four guarding Angels and a circle of fire. The cocoon of light provides you with magnetism. You are magnetic to positive, loving people, harmonious situations and experiences that reflect your highest spiritual potential, but your magnetism also deflects anything that may be inappropriate, negative or destructive for you. The Angels are there to defend you, guide you to safety and sharpen your senses, especially your intuition. The circle of fire strengthens and consolidates your power in a way that allows you to create appropriate boundaries in all of your relationships.

You may also ask for Angelic protection for someone you care about. If, for example, you know that your

Exercise continued

teenage son is feeling scared about something or is going to be out late at night, then you could simply imagine him cocooned in light and guarded by his Angels. You do not even need to tell him that you are doing this. Once you have asked the Angels for their assistance, do your best to let go and relax. You do not help yourself or the object of your concern by surrounding them with thoughts of worry. Instead, surround them with thoughts of love and offer any practical assistance that is appropriate.

Once you have completed this exercise, open your eyes and thank the Angels for their ongoing protection. You may find it helpful to repeat this process on a regular basis.

Exercise • End

SPIRITUAL HEALING

Many cultures, religions and spiritual philosophies have traditions of spiritual healing. The widest definition of spiritual healing is any process of healing, whether physical, mental or emotional, that has been facilitated by spiritual means. This would include any healing practice that allows for an exchange of spiritual energy between the healer and the recipient. Exchanges of this kind are invariably subject to Angelic intervention. Indeed, many health care professionals, both medical and complementary, unconsciously engage in forms of spiritual healing that are Angel blessed. For example, a dental nurse with natural healing abilities may act as a channel for Angelic healing energy. The dental nurse in question may be unaware of what she or he is doing but clients visiting the dental practice may feel calmer and more relaxed when this particular person is on duty. In some cases, the healing rate that occurs after dental operations may be greatly increased because the presence of this nurse has stimulated the patients' capacity for self-healing.

Healing is a natural human gift that lies dormant within us all, just waiting to be developed.

In my experience, many nurses and health care professionals have pronounced spiritual healing abilities. Healing is a natural human gift that lies dormant within us all. We all have the potential to develop as spiritual healers and those of us who are drawn to the caring professions often do so because our healing potential is particularly strong. If you wish to strengthen and enhance your natural healing abilities you could achieve this in a number of ways. You may choose to train in a physical therapy such as massage or reflexology or you may wish to focus upon the mind and emotions by taking a counselling course. Those who feel drawn to specialise in a form of complementary medicine may train in acupuncture, homeopathy, herbalism, osteopathy or one of a number of other disciplines. The list of healing therapies that may be a vehicle for spiritual healing is endless. Working with any of these skills will allow for an exchange of healing energy, particularly if you regularly ask the Angels to bless your clients with healing of the spirit. Alternatively you may wish to take a more direct route by training as a spiritual healer.

There are strong healing traditions in Europe, America and Australia that include practices of hands-on healing, touch healing or auric healing. As the terms suggest, hands-on healing and touch healing tend to utilise physical contact between healer and recipient, auric healing may not. Instead, an auric healer may focus upon the aura or electromagnetic field that exists around the human body. In recent times, forms of Asian spiritual healing such as Japanese Reiki have become increasingly popular in the western world. In truth, the exchange of spiritual healing is essentially similar, regardless of the approach, the theory or the techniques used. The differences come from the personal energy of the individual healer, the divine purpose of the guiding Angels and the specific needs of the clients.

*Spiritual healing may have a miraculous effect
upon the body's natural healing responses.*

When healing of the spirit occurs there is often a chain reaction that spreads throughout the entire human system.

What begins with the spirit may spread to the mind, then to
the emotions and finally to the body in the form of physical
relaxation, an adjustment of the immune response or
tangible physical healing. Receiving spiritual healing on a
regular basis may have a miraculous effect upon the body's
natural healing abilities, especially when teamed with
appropriate medical or complementary therapies. Even when
very little physical healing can occur, spiritual healing may
make an extraordinary difference by transforming other
areas of human consciousness. For individuals with long-
term medical conditions, regular spiritual healing may help
them come to terms with their condition and be better able to
manage their symptoms on a daily basis. It can be used as
part of a pain control programme as well as a tool for slowing
down physical deterioration and promoting a positive mental
vision of the future. Angels work alongside spiritual healers
because they wish to relieve suffering whenever possible.

Looking back at my childhood I can see that the Angels
were preparing me, with my unconscious consent, to be a
channel for spiritual healing. I was quite young when I first
realised that I often knew what other people were thinking
and feeling. This ability could be both valuable and
disturbing. It was useful to be able to read situations
effectively and know what was going on. Like most children,
I was often judged too young to understand the complexity of
adult moods and dramas, but I frequently understood more
than many of my elders. It could just occasionally be
disturbing to experience the unexpressed feelings of others. I
was often unsure whether it was my sadness I was feeling or
the sadness of someone who was around me. I sometimes still
experience this confusion, but I soon learned that if I thought
positively and lovingly about other people, their mood would
often change and they would begin to feel better. As a result,
I would feel better too.

Angels can teach us to work with them as healers,
channels and vehicles for spiritual guidance.

As a young adult, I discovered that I was a natural counsellor and although I first trained as an actor, I was also a voluntary counsellor working with a couple of agencies close to where I lived in the English Midlands. My theatrical work also became a focus for my healing development. While preparing to go on stage, my fellow performers and I would relax by giving each other back, neck and head massages. Whenever it was my turn to offer massage, I invariably had a longer queue of people waiting than anyone else. Most people who came to me relaxed very effectively and felt more emotionally balanced before the performance because of it. At the time, neither they, nor I, knew why this was the case. We probably all assumed that I was just better at kneading and loosening the knots than most. I now realise that my hands were guided by my healing Angels and that I was a vehicle for the spiritual energy they channelled through me.

It was only a couple of years later that a voice in my head told me I had healing ability and that I was to begin to call myself a healer. At the time I was not completely sure what it meant to be a healer. I was unsure of how to proceed or what the work would entail. Now I simply define a healer as someone who creates the space for other people to heal themselves. Perhaps, more accurately, I could say that a healer is someone who acts as a vehicle for the Angels to create a healing space, so that they may fill it with the love and light of the divine.

My first conscious attempts at hands-on healing were a revelation. I did not really know what I was doing, but a healing Angel stepped into my body and started to move my hands. It was as if this healing guardian was wearing me like a glove and very gently guiding my movements. My hands were directed to the areas of my client's body which most needed to receive the light that was being channelled through them. This happened again on a number of occasions until my Angels decided that I knew what I was doing and, like all gracious teachers, they stepped to one side to allow me to develop my own style. They still work alongside me as I heal, teach and write.

You may begin to operate as a spiritual healer by
asking the Angels to send healing light to everyone
you know, yourself included.

If you wish to be a spiritual healer, you can begin now by simply asking the Angels to send healing light to everyone you know. Remember to include yourself when you ask the Angels for healing. The best healers are those who learn to receive support as well as give it. To be a skilled spiritual healer takes time, training and life experience, but there are many good teachers, courses and books in the world that may assist you. Introductory techniques to help you develop your healing abilities can be found in my book, *Principles of Your Psychic Potential*. However, you may wish to start by inviting the Angels to transform your life and by sending 'absent' or 'distant' healing to anyone who you feel may need a boost of healing energy. The following ideas, invocations and exercises will help.

BECOMING MAGNETIC FOR ANGELIC HEALING

When you are sick, feeling lonely, feeling depressed or lacking energy and unable to motivate yourself, you may wish to ask the Angels for their healing support. You may also choose to do this when you are preparing for, or recuperating from, an operation. Just imagine your body, mind, emotions and spirit becoming magnetic for Angelic healing and ask your Angelic guardians to intervene by directing healing energy to wherever it is needed. You could imagine your Angels placing hands, wings or beams of healing light energy upon any area of your body that is in need of a healing boost or simply picture them radiating light directly to your mind, spirit or emotions. Do this regularly. If you are lying in bed recovering from an illness or an accident, you could even do this several times every day. Just remember that the more you ask, the more you will receive.

Talk to your Angels. If you can, be specific about your needs. You could ask them to bring you the healing that would help you evolve spiritually; you could ask them to comfort you during times of grief or heal the cause of your distress. You could even ask them to help your doctor, healer or complementary therapist provide the best available treatment for your condition. What is more, if you wish to develop your own healing abilities to help other people, you could ask your Angels for their guidance. When asked, Angels love to point you towards the right books, courses and tutors to build and enhance your skills in the best way possible. All you need to do is say,

'Angels, I need to find the perfect book about .... Please guide me in the right direction.'

Whatever your needs, you may increase your magnetism for Angelic healing by regularly using these affirmations.

Affirmations and Invocations

ATTRACTING ANGELIC HEALING

- I am now available for Angelic healing.
- The love of the Angels tranforms my life for the better.
- My Angels guide me to the perfect healer/doctor/counsellor/therapist for my needs.
- I allow the Angels to heal my spirit.
- I am magnetic for healing guides and Angels.
- I always receive the healing guidance I need.
- The Angels support me in physical, emotional and mental health.
- My spirit grows in wholeness.
- The light of healing shines from within me.
- I am always healthy, whole and complete.

- **Sending Angelic Healing**

Exercise

Once again, find a quiet, comfortable place to sit and relax. Breathe deeply, allow your eyes to close and use your imagination to contact the Angels of healing. You may ask for healing for someone who is sick, someone who is lonely or isolated, someone who is grieving or for any human need that another person may have. You may even send healing thoughts to someone who is quite well but who you instinctively feel may need a boost of confidence, joy or inspiration.

Begin by thinking of the person whom you wish to send Angelic healing. You do not have to know them intimately or even know their name, just focus upon the information you have about them and trust the Angels to make the connection with the right person. If you do know this person well, then take a few moments to think of them, remembering how they look or how it feels to be in their company as well as acknowledging their current situation. Ask the Angels to surround this individual with healing energy and provide them with the love and support required to facilitate a process of spiritual transformation.

Picture this person surrounded by Angels of healing. Each Angel has a special gift to bring. Some may cheer and comfort; some may offer protection while others may bathe this individual with golden rays of healing light. If there is physical illness or disease, imagine the light creating balance and harmony throughout the body. If there is emotional distress, the light calms and brightens the emotions and brings a new sense of hope. If this person is recovering from an accident, imagine the Angels using the light to disperse the fear and shock that may surround them and picture all breaks, sprains, burns or bruises healing rapidly.

Exercise continued Do your best to be as detached about the outcome as possible. When you are engaged in absent healing, it is not always possible to receive direct confirmation of effectiveness. Be content to send healing thoughts, ask for the help of the Angels and trust that the person in question will receive some healing or comfort. The form that this healing may take will vary and so will the results. All we can do is ask for the Angels to intervene, send our loving thoughts and surrender to the will of the divine. If there is any practical support to be offered, you will be guided to do so. **Exercise • End**

═══ INVOCATION ═══

Angels of Healing and Protection

May the Angels bless me with divine protection.

May the healing love of the Angels surround me wherever I go.

I ask that I may be a vehicle for spiritual healing.

I ask that I may receive Angelic healing on a daily basis.

My spirit is constantly healed by ministering Angels.

My guardian Angels always guide me to the healers, doctors and therapists that can best help me.

I thank my Angels for their transformative influence upon my soul.

I ask that I may learn to heal myself, become more positive and evolve spiritually.

I ask that I may bless the lives of others with the healing and protection of the Angels.

Chapter Seven
Being an Angel

Being an Angel is your destiny, your divine
purpose,
As you regain your memory,
You will know the truth of this,
Being an Angel is your first nature,
Being human, your second,
You wear humanity like a glove,
And ride through life like a child at a funfair,

You are a Star Seed dropped from the heavens,
Into the warm, fertile earth below,
Your purpose is to grow back towards the heavens,
And in doing so,
Transform everything you touch,
And transport this planet a little closer to the stars
above,

When you turn your face to the light,
And love your humanity in all its glory,
And all its confusion,
Then your human qualities will transform,
Your heart will be Angelic,
And love will reign supreme.

                              David Lawson, 1998

A COMPANY OF ANGELS

I decided to call my Angel course *A Company of Angels* for three reasons. First this title popped into my head unexpectedly; it seemingly arrived from nowhere and was not overtly connected to the train of thought I was having at the time. Indeed, I was more concerned with what I was going to have for lunch than with planning my future projects. Secondly, I then remembered that there are references to Angels in Judaic and Christian texts as the 'company of divine beings', so it seemed apt to pay tribute to this ancient concept. However, the most important reason for naming my course in this way was that I thought of it as an invitation. If I invited people to join me for *A Company of Angels* then I was sure the individuals who would respond to my invitation would be powerfully Angelic in nature, whether or not they were consciously aware of the fact. I was right. What is more, my invitation turned out to be doubly effective because, in addition to these Angels in training, my courses have been filled with the powerful Angelic presence of the many guiding spirits who have accompanied them.

A company of Angels is a grouping of individuals with a combined Angelic purpose.

As I have previously stated, my own definition of 'a company of Angels' is any grouping of two or more individuals who gather together to fulfil a greater Angelic purpose. By 'gather together' I do not mean that the individuals always have to be together in the same geographical location, although this can often be an important prerequisite for the Angelic purpose in question if it is dependent upon direct human interaction for its success. For example, a self-help group that meets on a weekly basis may have an Angelic purpose that includes mutual support. This support can often be best achieved by regular human contact where participants are able to learn from each other, share insights and offer emotional understanding. However, there are some Angelic gatherings that exist at a distance through the written word, telephone contact, communication over the Internet and through something that is both more powerful and more subtle — the communication that exists on the higher mental levels.

When we meditate, pray, daydream, sleep or instinctively follow a particular spiritual path, we are often connecting with other individuals who have a similar Angelic purpose to our own. Subtle telepathic communication exists between us all whether we are consciously aware of it or not. The same basic principles apply to all the connections we make whether they are in the higher mental and spiritual realms or in our normal waking reality. Birds of a feather flock together. Our individual dreams, desires and aspirations connect us to the dreams, desires and aspirations of others and so form a collective consciousness or 'group mind' that can have a powerful impact upon the world in which we live.

You may already be a member of a company of Angels.

I believe that many projects exist because some part of the group mind has called for them and the Angels have responded by motivating individual human beings to answer that call with their skills and creativity. Perhaps this book is such a project and you are one of a number of individuals who are part of a company of Angels with a purpose to bring greater Angelic consciousness into the world. The best way to achieve this purpose would be to strengthen your connection to your own guardian Angels and fully awaken your own Angelic potential. It is not the precise nature of my ideas and opinions that are most important in this, instead it is the inner knowing that my words may awaken in you that will facilitate this purpose. They are a little like a secret code that holds the key to some of the special gifts, skills and knowledge that the Angels have already planted within you.

WORKING WITH THE GROUP MIND

All things can be achieved with the support of the group mind, or collective consciousness. If you wish to build a

successful business, your success is more likely to be assured
if you work in harmony with the group mind of the
community that your business is serving. If the local
community needs a food store and you decide to open a shop
that sells hardware, you are not necessarily in tune with the
group mind and your business has less chance of success.
Similarly, your team of colleagues or employees who work
with you in your business will have a collective consciousness
that can be harnessed positively. Your success may be partly
dependent upon engendering a good team spirit amongst
your staff and upon encouraging individuals to feel that they
can make a positive and stimulating contribution. If your
staff feel that they are appreciated, if they have common
goals to work towards and a sense that they are sharing in
the success that they are helping to create, then the potential
for achievement is greatly enhanced.

When you invite the support of other people, you are
tapping into the power of the group mind.

Another way of tapping into the group mind is to ask for
help. Many people love to help if they can. It allows them to
express their Angelic nature and to feel that they are making
a positive difference to the world around them. Many of us
have learnt to deny our needs and not bother other people
with them, so we often give up seeking help when we receive
our first refusal. People rarely refuse to help because they
actively wish to deny help to you. They just say no because
they are tired or busy or because they lack the skills and
awareness required to address your particular needs at that
time. Those of us who work most effectively with the group
mind are often willing to ask many people for their support.
Perhaps the first two or three may refuse but the fourth may
come up with a brilliant idea and the fifth may follow up with
an offer of practical assistance. If you are looking for a new
place to live, tell all your friends, tell your colleagues at work
and tell the woman you meet at the bus stop every morning.
The more people who know, the more chance you will have of
achieving your goal.

Our Angels may assist us by helping us to operate in harmony with the group mind of family, friends, colleagues or community. When asked, they can help align our individual goals and spiritual potential with those of the group, in ways that are mutually beneficial for all concerned. They may also guide us to work with the group mind in the appropriate way to ensure success. When you are sailing down a fast-flowing river, it is generally easier to travel with the currents rather than push against them. Similarly, our Angels can help us to work with the purpose and momentum that is already there so that we can both contribute to the spiritual development of the group as well as benefit from it. It helps to have an intention to create a win-win situation with other people wherever possible, rather than operate from the assumption that in every relationship or transaction there has to be a loser.

The Angels may help us to work in harmony with the group mind.

The Angels can help us to work with the group mind in many practical ways. When we talk to our Angels, ask them for their help and ask that we may be guided towards like-minded people, they do their best to set things up for us. Seemingly chance meetings will be arranged between people who can positively contribute to each other's lives. Indeed, I have known people who have moved into a wonderful new home by asking their Angels to help them find the ideal place to live, in an environment where they may be surrounded by others with similar interests. In some cases, this has happened immediately, in ways that were easy to predict. In other instances, it has taken longer to achieve or has manifested in an unexpected form. For example, we may be guided to the perfect home environment, living near people who have a similar spiritual purpose to our own but in a geographical location that we had not previously considered. The Angels can only help us in ways that are in line with our highest spiritual goals and needs.

• Tapping into the Group Mind

Exercise

Find a quiet, comfortable place to sit and relax. Take a few long, slow, deep breaths to settle yourself before you begin and allow your eyes to softly close. Once again, visualise yourself in a cocoon of golden light energy. Within your cocoon of gold you are filled with a sense of peace, strength and stability.

Ask your Angels to connect you to other people whose Angelic purpose complements your own. You could imagine that your cocoon of light increases in spiritual magnetism so that wherever you go you attract people with whom you share compatible goals, common interests and similar visions of the future. Picture your guardians taking you to a beautiful place that is filled with the higher minds of others on a similar spiritual path. You could visualise this as being like a beautiful garden filled with fragrant flowers or, alternatively, a palace of light that is filled with many golden bubbles of consciousness, including your own. Find the images or concepts that best suit you and imagine yourself mingling with the other souls, becoming strengthened in your own spiritual purpose as you strengthen and inspire those you touch.

Imagine yourself making arrangements with some of the other souls. If it is feasible and desirable for you to meet on the physical level, then sense yourself agreeing to connect with each other at some point in the future. You may be drawn to some of these people socially, through your work or in one of a multitude of other ways. The Angels will take care of the details. For now, just bathe in the bliss of higher consciousness that is created by so many spiritually compatible souls drawn together in one place.

Exercise continued

See yourself stepping away from this place and instead, take some time to focus upon the group mind of your family, friends or colleagues. Ask the Angels to give you guidance about this group mind, invite them to bring healing to the group and help you to work in harmony with the needs and purpose of this collective consciousness. You may visualise the group mind of your family as a school of brightly coloured fish swimming together in a clear turquoise ocean. You may picture the group mind of your social circle as a collection of beautiful butterflies or your colleagues as bees in a hive. Create whatever images make sense to you and develop them so that you imagine the individuals who make up the group becoming better able to function together and enhance the spiritual potential of all.

You may even talk to the mind of a group you are not yet part of, such as a new set of colleagues or the students and staff of a college course that you are about to enrol upon. In your thoughts, ask the group to welcome you and ask that you may be able to contribute something of value to the other group members. Tell your Angels that you are open to receive any guidance that will help you to function happily and successfully as part of this group for as long as it is spiritually beneficial. When you complete this exercise, make a note of any insights you receive.   **Exercise • End**

LOOK FOR THE MESSAGE

Whether our spiritual purpose draws us to groups or to individuals, I believe that every relationship in our lives can be the vehicle for Angelic messages. Angels of scripture and mythology were often represented as messengers, perhaps the most famous, in Christian teachings, being Archangel Gabriel, who visited Mary to tell her that she was going to be the mother of Jesus Christ. Angels delight in providing us with messages that will enhance our lives and every human opportunity is taken to convey those messages to us. All meetings between people have a message attached to them if only we are willing to look for the message and act upon it with love.

We are Angelic messengers. It is part of the divine
purpose of all human beings and Angels in
training.

The messages attached to relationships may be numerous and their meanings diverse. Some messages may be a simple confirmation that we are going in the right direction while others may be a profound confirmation that we are loved and cherished for ourselves alone. With our consent, often unconscious, Angels use each of us as a vehicle for the messages they wish other people to receive and, in turn, we too are the recipients of Angelic messages that others have been charged with bringing to us. This exchange of messages can be as simple as being in the right place at the right time to give directions to a motorist who has lost her way or as involved as providing others with valuable spiritual lessons. There are times when expressing our ideas or opinions will remind other people of their forgotten goals, visions and spiritual potential and there are instances when expressing our vulnerabilities will develop the strengths of those we love.

As a healer, teacher and natural intuitive, the messages I have had for other people have often been quite pronounced. In some cases it is simply the message of self-healing or self-love that I am teaching as part of a particular workshop or event. Sometimes it may be a psychic message that I receive for an individual. On occasion these messages have been so powerful that I have felt compelled to pass them on, even at times when I have been nervous about the other person's response. Gradually, I am learning that when a message is Angel blessed, it is usually well received. However, in all situations, those involved have had powerful messages for me too. Like most teachers, I probably learn more from my students than they from me.

CREATING AN ANGEL SUPPORT GROUP

You may consider forming an Angel support group with some friends to help you all strengthen your connection with the Angels and enhance your spiritual purpose. You could take turns to host or lead the group and you may vary the activities according to the changing needs and interests of those involved. At some meetings you could guide each other through exercises or meditations that would help you to tap into your Angelic guidance. On other occasions, you might combine your loving intentions to send Angelic healing to individuals in need of comfort or areas of the world in need of peace. You may share your experiences of Angelic intervention, exchange ideas and practise developing your intuitive abilities in a safe, supportive atmosphere. You may even wish to organise outings to courses or events of mutual interest or walks through beautiful countryside that is Angel blessed. There are many books on Angels, personal development or spiritual development that would give you ideas for exercises and activities. Please feel free to adapt the ideas and meditations I have shared with you here.

Ask the Angels to help you create a successful support group.

Support groups are successful when the needs, wishes and ideas of all the individuals involved are fully incorporated into the regular activities of the group. Take time to listen to each other, giving individual group members equal space to express themselves and contribute their unique insights, talents and abilities. If there are areas of conflict that arise within the group, do your best to talk about them honestly, meditate together and ask the Angels to guide you to a new state of peace, harmony and understanding. When individual members have learnt all they can from a group, they will probably leave to seek their learning or support from elsewhere. This is both natural and necessary. Some groups last for years, others just for a few weeks. If you wish to begin a group and you do not have friends who would be interested, ask the Angels to connect you to other people who would benefit from Angelic guidance and mutual support.

YOU ARE AN ANGEL IN TRAINING

As an Angel in training you will be guided to fulfil more and more of your spiritual potential. Sometimes that guidance will seem clear and at other times you may wonder if your Angelic guardians exist at all. We all experience periods of our lives when we feel spiritually alone, confused or rudderless. Even the most positive among us wake up some mornings feeling devoid of spiritual guidance, comfort and support. This does not mean that our Angels have flown away to leave us to fend for ourselves. Indeed, these are usually times when our guardians are doing the most they can to assist us. Sometimes it is just that we have become so entrenched in our old thinking patterns and emotional dramas that we have put up a barrier between ourselves and our source of greatest support. Often it is because we have simply forgotten to ask for help. These fluctuations of mood and faith can be part of the process of developing as a spiritual being on a human path.

There will be some days when you will be filled with the joy and lightness of Angelic awareness. You will feel in tune with your own spiritual potential and in touch with your Angelic guardians. I call these the 'beacon days', when our light is at its brightest, our vision is at its strongest, we have a clearer sense of our spiritual purpose and we are able to see the bigger picture of our lives. In addition, we may feel motivated, creatively inspired and emotionally fulfilled. It would be a mistake to hold onto these days and desperately attempt to be like this all the time, but if we make the most of them, enjoy them while they last and allow them to inspire us before graciously letting them go, then they will come again with greater frequency.

Make the most of your 'beacon days' for they will remind you of your spiritual origins and guide you towards your spiritual destiny.

As I have said before, being an Angel in training is not about living up to an outmoded religious or moral code. Angels do not deny their own needs and martyr themselves to the needs of others. Instead, they love themselves so much that they have an abundance of love to share. This is the basis of their service. Angels are like vessels that are so full of love it overflows and others may drink of it. The development of your Angelic potential comes from personal integrity, personal responsibility, humour, joy, spiritual learning and spiritual contribution. Being true to yourself is a core part of your spiritual purpose and so is personal happiness. I believe that we were created to be happy. Happy people engender happiness in others. Those who love themselves bring more love to the world for everyone to share.

Affirmations and Invocations

AWAKENING THE ANGEL WITHIN

- It is safe and easy for me to become more Angelic.

- My Angelic awareness shines from within.

- I grow in love, light and divine purpose.

- I ask that I may make a positive contribution to the world.

- I love my humanity and embrace my Angelic brilliance.

- My Angels help me to grow by their example

- I was born from light and my light helps to transform the world.

- I now embark upon a wonderful, Angelic adventure.

- My career, relationships and life experiences all enhance my spiritual development.

- I am an Angel; I unfold my wings and fly.

• Being an Angel

Exercise

Find a quiet, comfortable place to sit and relax. Make sure that you are not going to be disturbed and take a few long, slow, deep breaths to settle yourself before you begin. Read through this exercise a couple of times to familiarise yourself with the key points before proceeding. Allow your eyes to softly close and use your imagination to paint the picture, build the feeling or frame the concept of the following sequence:

Exercise continued

Visualise yourself sitting by a beautiful pool. This is not a pool of water. Instead, it is filled with golden light in liquid form. A number of Angelic guardians are hovering near you to bring you assistance as you bathe in the pool and awaken your true Angelic nature. Picture yourself removing your clothing and stepping gently into the liquid light. The Angels support you as you walk into the sensual golden brilliance that is before you. As you immerse your body, imagine a feeling of warm acceptance and contentment spreading throughout you and see yourself beginning to change. It is as if the very cells of your body are transforming, reverting to their true Angelic nature and then evolving to assume their greatest spiritual potential.

In your mind, repeat to yourself:

'I ask the Angels to awaken my true Angelic nature and enhance my Angelic qualities.'

'I ask that my Angelic blueprint be brought to life.'

Feel the pool refreshing you and imagine that your Angels soothe you with the soft balm of their voices. Hear their words of encouragement and reassurance and listen to their songs of love. The air about you is filled with the fragrances of jasmine and rose that kiss your nostrils, fill your lungs and transport you into an ecstasy of pleasurable feelings. When you are ready, have the Angels help you out of the pool and see yourself standing there shimmering with gold.

Invite one of your guardians to step into your body and awaken your Angelic blueprint further. Visualise this Angel walking into you and picture your two outlines blurring and combining for a few moments. Feel the cells of your body transforming more rapidly as you become all you were created to

Exercise continued

be. Imagine yourself aligning with your highest spiritual purpose and picture yourself as the embodiment of the Angel you were always intended to become. You may see your image begin to change as you visualise how you look as an Angel. Once this process is complete, imagine your guardian Angel moving to one side and stepping back, with the others, to enjoy your beauty.

Thank your Angels for their help and, if appropriate to dress at all, adorn yourself with new clothing that is comfortable and beautiful. Before bringing your attention back to your immediate environment, take a few moments to imagine yourself going about your daily life and affairs. You may still be visibly human to most people, but the body and face of an Angel shine out from within you for other Angels to see and your light inspires all who come into contact with you to align to their greatest spiritual potential.

Exercise • End

YOUR ANGELIC MISSION STATEMENTS

We may take a lifetime, or longer, to explore all the facets of our spiritual purpose, but it certainly helps to ask the Angels for guidance about our true nature and divine mission. Using our imagination as a bridge once more, we can begin to create some Angelic mission statements to guide our present and future development. Mission statements are positive statements of purpose that are currently popular within business and management training. Small businesses and large corporations alike are utilising them as part of the package of personnel initiatives to motivate entire teams of individuals to work towards the core goals of the company.

Mission statements are positive statements of purpose, core values and spiritual intent.

When an organisation has mission statements, then all members of the team, from the boardroom to the shop floor, are clear about where they are aiming and they are better able to find the common ground between their own personal development and the development of the company. Within this context, mission statements may bring people together and harness the spiritual purpose of the company, even if that purpose is predominantly financial. However, many corporate mission statements focus upon excellence of service, quality of production and the care of clients and employees alike, rather than just on making a buck regardless of the human cost. The world of commerce is filled with Angelic souls who are expressing their love by doing the best job they know how.

On a personal level we may create mission statements to reflect our goals, spiritual principles and core values in all areas of our lives. We may have mission statements to remind us of our purpose within our family or our community as well those which help to guide us in our work, our recreation, our spiritual practices and our personal development. We can even formulate mission statements that will encourage us to take care of ourselves, take time out for relaxation and keep ourselves healthy. Mission statements act as declarations of intent and constant reminders of our highest aspirations, greatest potential for contribution and deepest desires.

When we keep our attention upon our mission statements, we may transform our lives.

We may carry our mission statements with us in our purse, wallet or briefcase so that we can refer to them often. Some people have their mission statements framed and hung upon the wall of their office. Others may have them pasted up by their bedside or printed on their business cards. An affirmation that we adopt as an ongoing declaration of our intent becomes a mission statement. Many of my well-used affirmations have grown into statements of personal mission. One example that has become a personal 'mantra' of focus, clarity and effectiveness is the affirmation, 'I do less to achieve more'. When I keep my attention focused upon this statement, it has an amazing effect upon my time management. It encourages me to make everything I do count. Some of the affirmations we have shared within this book may form the basis of Angelic mission statements or you may wish to originate statements yourself that express your unique Angelic purpose.

- ## Creating Your Mission Statements

Exercise

Take a piece of paper and a pen and write down a list of the things you feel most passionate about. What motivates you, what inspires you, what do you most love? Think of the times in your life when you feel most connected to your true feelings, greatest ideas and deepest wisdom and make reference to them. Do not dismiss any thoughts that come to your mind. Nothing is too big or too small to provide a valid base for your mission statements. Here are some examples to help you:

I feel passionate about:

My creative abilities

Making people laugh

My spiritual development

Healing the environment

Good Italian food

The dance of life

The colour orange

Travelling to new places

Healing my relationships

Exercise continued

Next, make a list of some of the things that you would like to achieve or create in your life. Include career goals, spiritual aims, emotional desires and visions of hope. Here are some examples to help you:

My goals, aims, desires and visions include:

> The development of my psychic and intuitive abilities
>
> A successful career in public relations
>
> Prosperity, harmony and health for my family
>
> A home that truly reflects my needs and unique creativity
>
> The ability to learn something valuable from each new experience
>
> A world that is safer to live in
>
> A growing sense of spiritual fulfilment
>
> New opportunities to contribute my special gifts and insights
>
> A chance to make a difference to the lives of those I meet

Take your time to write these lists. It may be valuable for you to put them down, do something entirely different for a while and go back to them later so that your mind can give you more information. You may even sleep with them beside your bed and ask your Angels to give you guidance as you sleep that will help you create your mission statements.

Exercise continued

Drawing from the information in your first two lists, begin to create some appropriate statements of personal mission. Our mission statements need to encompass the Angelic potential that is present within our passions and our goals for the future. What is more, they need to reflect our personal values in all key areas of our lives, including our health, our family, our careers, our friendships and our spiritual practice. Here are some examples:

My angelic mission on earth is ...

> to dance with the magic of life.

> to respect the rhythms of nature.

> to express my inner wisdom.

> to treat everyone in my life with the greatest respect, myself included.

> to enjoy the colour, sensuality and spirit of the world around me

> to bring love and spiritual guidance into the lives of other people

> to be a successful businessman/woman working ethically and profitably for the good of all concerned

> to heal myself and bring healing to my environment

> to always have a sense of humour

Review and refine your Angel mission statements on a regular basis. Some statements of personal mission may guide and inspire you for years to come while others may simply be a stepping stone

Exercise continued

to greater self awareness. Carry your Angelic mission statements with you, refer to them often and be creative in the ways you use them to express your intent. Thank you for reading this book and being part of *A Company of Angels*. May your Angelic mission carry you forward to wonderful new adventures.

End

Exercise •

═══════ INVOCATION ═══════

Being An Angel

May I be an Angel in everything I think, say and do.

May my light shine out to the world to bring hope and illumination.

I ask that I may grow in fun, joy and laughter.

I ask that I may be magnetic for others on a similar spiritual path.

My Angels guide and inspire me with every step of my journey.

My Angels love me as I shine my love to others.

Being an Angel, I heal myself.

Being an Angel, I help to heal the world.

I give thanks for the brilliance of my divine potential.

●●●●●●●●●●●●●●●●●●●●●●●●●●●●●●

INTRODUCING FINDHORN PRESS

Findhorn Press is the publishing business of the Findhorn
Community which has grown around the Findhorn Foundation,
co-founded in 1962 by Peter and Eileen Caddy and Dorothy
Maclean. The first books originated from the early interest in
Eileen's guidance over 25 years ago and Findhorn Press now
publishes not only Eileen Caddy's books of guidance and inspi-
rational material, but also many others. It has also forged links
with a number of like-minded authors and organisations.

For further information about the Findhorn Community and
how to participate in its programmes, please write to:

The Accommodation Secretary
Findhorn Foundation
Cluny Hill College
Forres IV36 0RD
Scotland
Tel. +44 (0)1309 673655 Fax +44 (0)1309 673113
e-mail: reception@findhorn.org
url: http://www.findhorn.org

For a complete catalogue or more information about Findhorn
Press products, please contact:

Findhorn Press
The Park, Findhorn, Forres IV36 0TZ, Scotland, or
P. O Box 13939, Tallahassee, Florida 32317-3939, USA
Tel. +44 (0)1309 690582 Fax +44 (0)1309 690036
e-mail: books@findhorn.org
url: http://www.findhorn.org/findhornpress/

●●●●●●●●●●●●●●●●●●●●●●●●●●●●

Introducing Eileen Caddy ...

Since the day in 1953 when Eileen Caddy first heard an inner voice say, 'Be still and know that I am God', she has not only lived her personal life by that inner guidance, but has also been instrumental in creating the international spiritual community centred around the Findhorn Foundation. Eileen realised that her role was to help others turn within and find their own inner direction and her books reflect this encouragement to us all. Eileen's books have sold hundreds of thousands of copies throughout the world, in more than 20 languages. She continues to live and work in the Findhorn Foundation.

Opening Doors Within

Eileen Caddy's most popular book – 365 pieces of guidance received during her meditations, one for each day of the year. They contain simple yet practical suggestions for living life with joy, inspiration and love. Translated into more than 20 languages, this treasure of a book is the perfect present for loved ones. Now available in both hardcover and paperback.

Pbk 404–pp   £6.95 • US$12.95   ISBN 0 905249 68 2
Hbk 404–pp   £10.95 • US$17.95   ISBN 0 905249 66 6

Waves of Spirit

Practical ways to face today's life challenges

Eileen's most recent book, with both guidance which comes through her, and wisdom and experience of Eileen the woman. She shares her challenges and struggles in life, and gives her perspectives on many major life questions we all share — forgiveness, sexuality, unconditional love, healing relationships, children and The Christ amongst them. This book is like a breath of fresh air to all seekers on the spiritual path who are trying to make sense of life in today's stressful world.

Pbk 144–pp   *£5.95 • US$10.95*   *ISBN 1 899171 75 4*

Judy Hall

from Astrology to Soulmates — and much more...

The Zodiac Pack:
A Visual Approach to Astrology

Have you ever wanted to learn how to lay out your own astrological chart and be able to interpret it yourself intuitively? The Zodiac Pack allows you to do just that, and whether you are a total beginner or have been working with Astrology for a lifetime, you will get something completely new from this unique tool. The beginner will find themselves being able to immediately learn more about themselves, using the beautiful cards to create a visual chart of their lives. The experienced Astrologer will find a new dimension added to their work, which will allow them work more intuitively with their clients.

Pack includes book: **Astrological Images** *(320–pp, fully illustrated),*

44 Full Colour Cards & Base Layout

£24.95 • US$34.95   ISBN 1 899171 85 1

Hands Across Time:

The Soulmate Enigma

Ask most people what they mean by soulmate and they will reply 'the person who makes me feel complete', or, 'my other half'. They are convinced that there is only one soulmate for them, and that when that soulmate comes into their life, it will bring them everything they have ever wished for — they will live happily ever after. For those who believe in reincarnation, this soulmate will be someone with whom they have shared life after life, almost certainly as lovers. But whilst this may happen, twenty years of exploring karmic relationships led Judy Hall to believe it is not that simple. A soulmate contact from one life may not carry over to the present life. The search for a soulmate, or the memory of a previous association, can so often wreck ordinary relationships. A better definition of a soulmate might be a soul companion who helps us to grow. This growth may entail some very hard lessons indeed, and our soulmate may just be the person with whom we go to hell and back — not as a punishment but as a learning process. Nor is the relationship necessarily for ever — it is for as long as it takes. What is more, we may have several soulmates with whom we have been in many different relationships in the past. Hands Across Time help us recognise the dangers and joys of searching for that special person to makes us feel complete.

Pbk 192–pp   *£6.95 • US$11.95*   *ISBN 1 899171 61 4*

The Art of Psychic Protection

- Do you meditate or in any other way seek to expand your consciousness?

- Are you a therapist or healer?

- Do you use self-hypnosis tapes?

- Do people come to you with their problems?

- Are you often tired, feeling hopeless and over-emotional?

- Are you accident-prone?

If you answer yes to any of the above, the chances are that you need psychic protection. This books covers the basic and highly practical tools for psychic protection, suitable for both groups and individuals. These techniques have been tried and tested, some dating back thousands of years while other belong to the twenty-first century. All can be learned quickly and will soon become an automatic part of life.

Pbk 144–pp   £5.95   ISBN 1 899171 36 3